VODKA

VODKA

How a Colorless, Odorless, Flavorless Spirit
Conquered America

Victorino Matus

Lyons Press
Guilford, Connecticut
An imprint of Rowman & Littlefield

Lyons Press is an imprint of Rowman & Littlefield.
Absolut® vodka, Absolut country of Sweden vodka & logo, Absolut,
Absolut bottle design, and Absolut calligraphy are trademarks
owned by the Absolut Company AB.

Frontispiece: Licensed by Shutterstock.com
Distributed by
NATIONAL BOOK NETWORK

Library of Congress Cataloging-in-Publication Data

Matus, Victorino.
 Vodka : how a colorless, odorless, flavorless spirit conquered America
/ Victorino Matus. — First edition.
     pages cm
 Summary: "How risk-taking entrepreneurs defied the odds and turned
medieval medicine into a multibillion-dollar industry"— Provided by
publisher.
 ISBN 978-0-7627-8699-2 (hardback)
 1. Vodka—United States. 2. Distilleries—United States. 3.
Distilling industries—United States. I. Title.
 TP607.V6M37 2014
 338.4'76635—dc23
                                                        2014015139

Printed in the United States of America

TO KATE

After the first glass of vodka
you can accept just about anything
of life even your own mysteriousness

—FRANK O'HARA, "AS PLANNED"

CONTENTS

INTRODUCTION

I believe that if life gives you lemons, you should make lemonade . . . and try to find somebody whose life has given them vodka and have a party.

—Ron White

In the early morning hours of August 9, 2006, Maurice Clarett, a former Ohio State tailback, led police on a ten-minute car chase through Columbus, Ohio. Clarett had run over a spike strip, and his Hyundai Santa Fe hobbled into a restaurant parking lot where authorities surrounded him.

He was in the vicinity of a key witness scheduled to testify against him in an armed robbery trial. Officials suspected that he was trying to stop that from happening. Clarett screamed obscenities and resisted arrest. Officers fired tasers, but to no avail. He was wearing a bulletproof vest. They resorted to pepper spray, which worked, and then hauled him to jail.

According to the impound slip, Clarett's SUV contained an arsenal of three handguns and an AK-47 assault rifle. Also found in the vehicle were a box of Trojan condoms, $761 in cash, a diploma, two teddy bears, and an empty bottle of

< ix >

vodka. In a photo that went viral, you can see the unmistakable long neck and frosted glass bottle of Grey Goose resting on the passenger seat next to one of the handguns and the rifle. Clarett subsequently pleaded guilty to a variety of charges and was sentenced to seven and a half years in prison. Released on good behavior in 2010, Clarett now plays rugby and writes a blog.

In the early morning hours of February 18, 2012, a fistfight erupted inside the Double Seven nightclub in New York City's posh Meatpacking District. A group of mostly twentysomething socialites allegedly accosted a VIP table, insulting the women, who happened to be models, and helped themselves to their $450 table-service bottle of Grey Goose. At that point Adam Hock, one of the VIPs, took action. (Hock, a physically imposing figure, insists the boys started the fight.)

But Hock didn't know whom he was fighting: Vladimir Restoin Roitfeld, son of fashion designer and former editor in chief of *Vogue Paris* Carine Roitfeld; Stavros Niarchos, grandson of a Greek shipping magnate and one of Paris Hilton's ex-boyfriends; real estate investor Diego Marroquin; and finally, the fellow Hock knocked out cold: twenty-four-year-old Pierre Casiraghi, prince of Monaco and grandson of Grace Kelly.

"Pierre's face looked broken," said one witness.

Hock admitted to disorderly conduct, avoiding jail time. Not that it was a one-sided affair: One of the prince's

What more do you need? The interior of Maurice Clarett's SUV: Note the bottle of Grey Goose Vodka next to the AK-47.
Courtesy of the Columbus Division of Police

< x >

entourage tried hitting Hock over the head with a bottle of Grey Goose.

If we're not drinking vodka, we're taking it on a wild goose chase, so to speak, or using it as a club in a club. Whatever the method, we cannot get enough of it. Americans drink more vodka than any other spirit. It makes up 32 percent of the market; that's essentially one of every three cocktails, totaling more than $5 billion in supplier revenue.

According to the Distilled Spirits Council of the United States, Americans purchased more than sixty-five million cases of vodka in 2012, almost 155 million gallons of a liquid defined by the federal government as "without distinctive character, aroma, taste, or color." Yet over a thousand brands battle for market share. In 2012 alone, 171 new brands (and 122 flavors) came onto the market. That's one new vodka every two or three days. How did it come to this?

In the summer of 2011, I wrote a feature for the *Weekly Standard,* "Vodka Nation," with the aim of sorting this all out. But the deeper I delved, the more convoluted the industry appeared.

If vodka is flavorless, odorless, colorless, and without character, how can one brand distinguish itself from the rest? Can a vodka tout its purity and at the same time deliver a flavor, thereby creating a distinction? In the most narrow terms, the answer is yes. Aside from determining the vodka's base— corn, potatoes, grain, wheat, grapes, or beet sugar, which subtly affect taste and texture—the Alcohol and Tobacco Tax and Trade Bureau allows for the addition of sugar, provided "the sugar does not exceed two-tenths of 1 percent," and citric acid, so long as it is "only added in a 'trace amount' not to exceed 1,000 parts per million."

< xii >

That's what it comes down to in this multibillion-dollar industry: parts per million. Well, that and marketing. For instance, can a top-shelf vodka achieve high volume? Can it claim elite status yet be consumed by millions? It seems contradictory, but Grey Goose fits the bill, all thanks to marketing.

The strange thing about vodka's dominance is how it transpired so suddenly. For two centuries America drank brown spirits—from the colonial rum trade and the Whiskey Rebellion to the Bourbon Trail and Prohibition. But in 1934, just after Prohibition ended, the first vodka distillery in America opened in Bethel, Connecticut . . . and then almost closed down for lack of interest.

Yet by 1967 vodka overtook gin as the country's top clear spirit. (It helped that it was harder to detect on the breath.) Soon people were ordering vodka martinis, shaken, not stirred. In 1976, the bicentennial, vodka officially beat out whiskey, bourbon, and rum as the nation's favorite spirit. At the time, we drank mostly American vodkas, and, with the exception of Smirnoff, none of it was any good. But then came an absolutely ingenious bottle from Sweden, and everything changed.

To this day both advertising execs and laypeople alike regard the Absolut advertising campaign as one of the most successful and iconic ever run, all of it without the help of television commercials. Absolut transformed vodka into a status symbol. Suddenly people stopped asking for vodka tonics and requested Absolut by name; it had, in bartender parlance, become a call drink. Then Grey Goose arrived, and the ladies on *Sex and the City* began ordering Grey Goose Cosmos.

It was all image: a bottle rated "the world's best tasting vodka," which was distilled from the finest French wheat and

< xiii >

This billboard for Wódka understandably didn't go over well.
Courtesy of Todd Gutnick, Anti-Defamation League

filtered through Champagne limestone. Little did most people realize that the creator of Grey Goose lived in New Rochelle, New York, and his previous claim to fame was popularizing Jägermeister.

In 2005 the *New York Times* conducted a blind taste test featuring twenty-one craft and super-premium vodkas. But the organizer, Bernard Kirsch, slipped in a bottle of inexpensive Smirnoff. The interloper won unanimously. But you won't see anyone ordering Smirnoff for bottle service at a Las Vegas hot spot. Sin City's favorite vodka is Grey Goose. At the same time, Ohio's favorite vodka is Kamchatka, which sells for about $8.99. In 2010 residents of the Buckeye State purchased some four hundred thousand gallons of it. As one vodka distiller explained, there's room for everyone to grow.

< xiv >

But the struggle to set a brand apart can lead to tacky, if not desperate, measures: In November 2011 a lower-tier vodka—known in the industry as a value brand—ran head-first into accusations of anti-Semitism when it put up a billboard on Manhattan's West Side Highway that read CHRISTMAS QUALITY, HANUKKAH PRICING. The brand Wódka's motto is "Great Vodka. Priced Right," but the billboard depicted a Chihuahua in a Santa cap next to an Afghan hound wearing a yarmulke. It was all . . . a bit much.

Drinks writer Jason Wilson nearly lost it when he came across Rue 33, a vodka made by Sam's Club. "It is made in Cognac, France, just like Grey Goose, but true to Sam's Club's form, this six-time distilled, ultra-premium vodka will be sold, economy-sized, in 1.75-liter bottles," he writes in *Boozehound: On the Trail of the Rare, the Obscure, and the Overrated in Spirits*. Wilson imagines the boardroom decision making that led to Rue 33: "Let's create some booze we can sell two aisles over from the diapers and the kitty litter, in 1.75-liter containers, at the seemingly affordable yet actually ridiculous price point of twenty-eight dollars."

On the other end of the price spectrum stands G Spirits Vodka, which goes for $150 per half-liter bottle! What makes it so special? According to the brand's website, "We guarantee that every single drop was poured over the breasts of Evelin." Let's just say Evelin is an attractive model. (They even have the video to prove it!)

In *The King of Vodka,* Linda Himelstein's biography of Pyotr Smirnov, you will come across this analysis from Russia's Central Chemical Laboratory: "The product's reputation doesn't always depend on the quality. . . . Very often,

< xv >

the product's reputation depends on its harmonious name, bottle's shape, colorful label, or just a more expensive price of the product." This observation was made around 1901.

Has anything changed?

Craft distillers are making vodka, even flavored ones, within the narrow parameters of the government's official definition. A number of these microdistillers do their own fermenting, too. (The majority of vodka makers import their neutral grain spirits from a handful of ethanol contract manufacturers.) Some of the large companies also describe themselves as craft distillers . . . that just happened to do *really* well.

I traveled across the country, visiting distillers large and small, craft and corporate alike, trying to make sense of it all. I flew to California to see SKYY, a brand fighting to get back on the top shelf; Anchor Distilling, where I witnessed the creation of a new vodka; and St. George Spirits, one of the early craft pioneers, which came up with Hangar One (and, yes, it's made inside a hangar).

I sat on a porch with Tito Beveridge, maker of Tito's Handmade Vodka, looking out onto the brown hills and scrub brush of Texas—and, yes, that's his real name. The man failed at five different jobs before succeeding in vodka. But it wasn't easy at first. He spent many nights alone with his dog next to his still. His friends told him to give it up, but he persevered.

In Deerfield, Illinois, I interviewed a corporate honcho at Jim Beam, whose second biggest-selling product turns out to be vodka, a brand that comes in thirty flavors, including Strawberry Shortcake and Rainbow Sherbet. (I offered my own flavor suggestion, which made his jaw drop.) Then I

< xvi >

drove up through Wisconsin farmland to visit a craft distillery so successful that it may no longer qualify as craft.

In New York I stumbled across an unlikely band of vodka entrepreneurs known as Industry City Distillery and sat with the modern-day Mad Men at TBWA, the ad agency behind Absolut. In a SoHo studio, I had coffee with a painter whose works the Smithsonian and Metropolitan Museum of Art have collected, and asked him how he ended up designing the skull for Dan Aykroyd's Crystal Head Vodka.

In Holland I toured the Ketel One plant, shoveled a hunk of coal under the pot-still, and watched a movie inside a windmill. In Las Vegas, for the Nightclub & Bar Show, I was offered (at a club) my own booth with bottle service for a mere $3,000.

How and why did this neutral grain spirit come to dominate our culture? Who made vodka what it is today? It starts with a friend who dropped everything to pursue the American Dream—in this case the dream of having your own brand of vodka.

< xvii >

VODKA

1

"A PLUNGE OFF THE VERY DEEP END"

When I sell liquor, it's called bootlegging; when my patrons serve it on Lake Shore Drive, it's called hospitality.

—AL CAPONE

Chicagoans have always had a fondness for booze—Billy Sunday notwithstanding—so it came as a surprise to learn that, since Prohibition ended in 1933, no distillery had opened within the city limits until 2008. But it was even more astonishing to learn that the person who started it was an Austrian friend from Washington, DC, Robert Birnecker.

I first encountered Birnecker in 2005 when my wife and I were planning a trip to Vienna and I asked the Austrian Embassy for restaurant recommendations. (What, they have something better to do?) Robert and a few other staffers at the press and culture desk assembled and e-mailed what turned out to be a great list. Some time later, he and I had lunch in Washington. He said that he had met a nice girl, and it was getting serious. Soon after, he married Sonat

< 1 >

Hart, a professor of German literature and Jewish studies. She taught in Baltimore, and he worked at the embassy. They had their first son, Lion, in 2008. Life was good—and stable. Then Robert left his job as deputy press secretary, and Sonat quit teaching. They moved to Chicago to open a distillery.

Vodka has this effect on people.

What makes someone abandon the safety and security of a diplomatic or academic position in order to build a distillery from the ground up and compete in an already crowded market against better-financed brands? Why make yet another flavorless, odorless, colorless substance and have to somehow find a way to differentiate yourself from a thousand others?

They certainly weren't alone in making that dramatic shift. People from all walks of life—Wall Street bankers, mortgage realtors, economics majors, artists, actors—have dropped what they were doing to make alcohol for a living. In *The Age of Gold: The California Gold Rush and the New American Dream,* historian H. W. Brands quotes Franklin Buck, a New York merchant, struck with gold fever:

> *When I see business firms—rich men—going into it, men who know how to make money, too, and young men of my acquaintance leaving good situations and fitting themselves out with arms and ammunition, tents, provisions and mining implements, there is something about it—the excitement, the crossing the Isthmus, seeing new countries and the prospect of making a fortune in a few years—that takes hold of my imagination, that tells me "Now is your chance. Strike while the iron is hot!"*

Was the iron still hot, or was it, as one industry insider told me, Sutter's Mill in 1850?

Robert and Sonat Birnecker faced considerable challenges. First, they were starting from scratch. They found space in Chicago's Ravenswood neighborhood, seven miles north of downtown. The copper pot and column stills arrived in sections from Germany, at a considerable cost. Most daunting of all, though, they were building the first legal distillery in Chicago, albeit a boutique distillery and not anything like the massive Smirnoff facility some forty miles southwest in Plainfield.

Robert and Sonat Birnecker. *Courtesy of Koval*

< 3 >

To be honest, they didn't go into the business to make vodka. They wanted to make fruit brandies (more eau-de-vie than schnapps) and whiskeys. But these take time. Fruits are seasonal, and whiskeys need barrel aging. They couldn't just sit on product without a moving revenue stream. Since it takes no time to process and composes 32 percent of the market, vodka, recommended by their distributor, became the obvious solution.

The Birneckers did have two points in their favor. Sonat originally hails from Chicago, and she knows the city well. The location they chose for their new venture turned out to be perfect—safe, quiet, and only two blocks from the bars and restaurants of Clark Street. Second, Robert comes from a distilling family. Expertise and advice lay only a phone call away. Robert's grandfather actually flew over from Austria to help. But everything else—including navigating thousands of pages of federal, state, and local regulations—they had to learn on their own.

The distillery is called Koval, a Yiddish term for a black-smith as well as a black sheep of the family. (One of Sonat's great-grandfathers left Vienna for Chicago in the early 1900s, and one of Robert's grandfathers is a Schmid, the German word for smith.) In 2011 they had four employees on the payroll, a gift shop, and—importantly—a tasting room made possible by Sonat's legal efforts to press Illinois to issue a separate license to *craft* distillers that allowed for such a space. Not far from the stills and vats stood a playpen for Lion and a second son, Rye. (One booze blogger wondered if they planned to name a third child Spelt.) A child's desk sits next to the grown-ups' table, which Robert calls his son's office.

By now, the whiskeys have come of age, and the place is buzzing. In 2011 Koval sold five thousand cases of spirits, mostly whiskey. But the share of vodka had declined from 40 percent to 10 percent of their overall output. There's nothing wrong with the vodka. It's flavorful, rye-based, twice distilled, and then filtered. Robert insists on pointing out that his vodka is 100 percent rye. By law, a spirit need only be 51 percent rye to be called rye whiskey. Other brands won't tell you anything about their composition; those usually just say "distilled from grain."

"Most vodkas on the market, I believe, are distilled from corn or wheat or a blend thereof primarily because those are the cheapest grains," says Meg Bell, Koval's brand ambassador in 2011. "It's a little silly to buy a bunch of grapes and make it into vodka. Why buy the most expensive material to turn into a neutral spirit?" For one, if you're Ciroc, which does exactly that and has the backing of Sean Combs—current stage name P. Diddy—it's going to sell really well.

"Here's the problem with the vodka market," Robert explains. "We may have a very good vodka, but there are a lot of other forces out there on levels where we can't compete, in terms of what distributors are able to give bars for using a certain vodka. A lot of it is pay-to-play. I know companies that, if you buy five cases of this flavored vodka, you get two cases or one case of the unflavored vodka for free."

Sometimes the interaction between distributor and retailer turns into outright bribery. Following a three-year

Koval Vodka in its
latest form.
Courtesy of Koval

investigation, the Alcohol and Tobacco Tax and Trade Bureau fined ten distributors for violating the Federal Alcohol Administration Act. A release from January 2009 described such illegal activities as "furnishing or giving money or other things of value to a retailer . . . and/or paying or crediting the retailer for advertising and/or preferred shelf space." Fines totaled $803,000.

Some things Koval simply cannot do.

In fact, Michael Roper, owner of the nearby Hopleaf Bar, remembers when he first came across the upstart distillers. "Sonat went up and down Clark Street with the baby carriage, and there were bottles underneath, where most people put their diapers and stuff, and she came in here in the afternoon. It's like someone coming in saying, 'You want to try some of our applesauce?' but instead: 'You want to try our vodka?'" he says with a laugh. "It was very, very homespun, and you know, they didn't do this throughout their area, but we're

< 6 >

only a couple of blocks away, so they sold it to us as like a neighborhood thing, and it was kind of fun."

But Robert admits to neglecting vodka in favor of his expanding portfolio, which includes white whiskey, aged whiskey, rye, and liqueurs (including rose hip and ginger). Barrels need filling, but he's also running out of storage space. He's planning to expand operations, and he and his team conduct distillation seminars several times a year to boost revenue. During my visit, a package arrived. A fellow distiller had sent Robert a jar of white whiskey along with a note asking him to figure out what was wrong with it.

There's no doubt that Robert spends more time at work than he ever did at the embassy. Does he have regrets? "I should've left sooner," he jokes. "Honestly, we liked our old jobs. I liked being at the embassy. My wife liked being a professor. It was good. . . . D.C. is not the worst place to live in." That said, "We wanted, first of all, to be able to work together, and we wanted to manufacture something. We looked at all kinds of other possibilities and we said, well, this is something we know from my family heritage, where we know how to produce something at a very high quality, where we wanted to be. We can work together. And it's something this country is missing. Chicago didn't have a distillery at the time. . . . It all came together."

But Robert adds that their venture was far from a sure thing: "In November 2008 I thought this was definitely a plunge off the very deep end. We had no production. We had rent to pay. We were still negotiating with distributors because producing the product is one thing, getting it sold is another. At that point it was just me. Sonat had the kid, and I was working at the distillery all alone and not getting where I wanted to be." The brandy had to wait because they had just missed the fruit season. "So we said we can't wait a year and sit around and do nothing. We have to start with grains. Then we said, okay, we'll do white whiskeys, vodka, and liqueurs. That wasn't easy to develop. . . . We were lucky with the rose hip and the ginger. Those two took off immediately, and the

Koval Bourbon and White Whiskey. *Courtesy of Koval*

< 8 >

rye vodka worked from the start, and so did our two white whiskeys."

Something resembling a look of fear comes over his face as he recalls that dark time. "Oh, there were moments. There were definitely moments where it was like, This is not going to work out. But," he sighs with relief, "we were very fortunate."

Not everyone is. Some have the know-how but not the money (microdistillers). Others have money but no savvy (Trump Vodka). Those who succeed have both, plus lots of luck and the courage to take that "plunge off the very deep end." It's been the same story for centuries.

2

VODKI

But give vodka to this peasant, and he is entirely changed.
He becomes quarrelsome and violent.

—*New York Times*, June 28, 1914

October 4 is National Vodka Day, but no one knows precisely when, where, or even why vodka was first made. (Even NationalVodkaDay.com admits that "we have not found the origins of why, but it works for us. No harm celebrating responsibly on other days as well.") It depends on your definition of vodka.

We can go as far back as the eighth century AD, when alchemist Jabir ibn Hayyan, known to the West as Geber, invented the alembic to capture vapor from heated wine, which he described as "of little use, but of great importance to science." (If only he had placed it in a frosted glass bottle and had beautiful women sell it at the local taverns!) In the fourteenth century, the Italians were drinking *aqua vitae*, which supposedly they learned to make from alchemists in southern France, who, in turn, had studied the methods of the Arabs. In any event the Italians brought their product to Moscow, and around 1430 a Russian monk named Isidore supposedly turned this into vodka.

That liquid nowhere near resembled the neutral grain spirits we drink today. It smelled bad, tasted worse, and was more medicinal in nature, probably best applied topically than ingested. (Even in more recent times, a friend reports that when she fell sick in Tashkent the local doctor told her to take some vodka . . . and rub it on her chest.) But over the centuries, distillation methods improved, and vodka—the word most likely a diminutive of the Russian word for water, воды, or, in the Roman alphabet, *voda*—became the drink of choice in the Russian Empire.

But far from being used to "celebrate responsibly," all levels of society abused it heavily. In the 1690s, for instance, Peter the Great founded his All Drunken, All-Jesting Assembly, which devoted itself to mocking the Orthodox church. The czar also invented the "penalty shot," described in *Ria Novosti* as "a shot of vodka that those who arrived late for a feast were forced to drink. In fact, when he organised feasts, the penalty shot came in the form of a 1.5-litre goblet named the Big Eagle." Peter proved less tolerant outside his court, however, forcing those caught publicly intoxicated to wear a fifteen-pound medal of shame for a week.

By the nineteenth century, vodka had become the principal source of tax revenue for the Russian government, as much as 46 percent of the budget. Alcoholism ran rampant. One estimate tallied two hundred thousand vodka-related deaths per year. A burgeoning temperance movement

Peter the Great, vodka drinker as depicted by William Faithorne II.
Courtesy of the Hubbard Collection, Library of Congress

included Anton Chekhov and Leo Tolstoy. The government found itself in an untenable position: in need of the money from vodka sales but dealing with a degenerating society. A solution came in the form of the Guardianship of Public Sobriety in 1895 and the State Vodka Monopoly, created a year later. Both were total disasters.

< 13 >

"Alcohol, Death, and the Devil" by George Cruikshank.
Courtesy of the Library of Congress

In *The Alcoholic Empire: Vodka and Politics in Late Imperial Russia,* author Patricia Herlihy explains how "the state attempted to confine the sale of alcoholic beverages to government-run stores where no food was served. After purchases in the state-controlled store, drinkers downed vodka on the street and smuggled vodka into *traktirs* (cheap eating establishments)." Worse, these regulated stores couldn't halt an ever-growing black market of watered-down or poison-infused vodkas. The guardianship, meanwhile, emphasized moderation rather than abstinence. Herlihy quotes the welfare

< 14 >

"King Alcohol and his Prime Minister" engraved by John Warner Barner.
Courtesy of the Library of Congress

"The Drunkard's Progress" (1846), from a glass with a friend to death by suicide, by N. Currier. *Courtesy of the Library of Congress*

institution's official goals as: "to create intelligent entertainment which might attract and raise the spiritual level of the population, widen its horizons, give it healthy nourishment, and care for its bodily health." The author, a professor of Russian and Soviet history and a vodka expert as well, adds that "the irony of the state's being the sole purveyor of alcohol while piously proclaiming moderation in drink was not lost on contemporaries."

But one good thing did come from this mess: a vodka of unprecedented purity using fresh ingredients distilled by a former serf named Pyotr Smirnov. He began in 1864, and by 1872, writes Linda Himelstein in *The King of Vodka*, "Smirnov employed more than sixty workers and oversaw

< 16 >

"Facing the Enemy" by F. W. Edmonds, engraving by T. Doney (1846).
Courtesy of the Library of Congress

three managers. He produced up to 100,000 pails of alcoholic drinks and grossed 600,000 rubles annually, or the equivalent of almost $7 million in today's dollars."

In 1876 the rising distiller brought his vodkas to the Centennial Exhibition in Philadelphia, where they won medals.[1] Himelstein cites the *New York Times*'s coverage, which pays prescient attention to packaging: "The first thing that strikes one is the variety of wines, brandies, and liqueurs Russia must

---

1 At the same Centennial, a gold medal also went to a light rum made by one Facundo Bacardi of Cuba.

< 17 >

Temperance Singers in New York by S. B. Morton (1874).
Courtesy of the Library of Congress

make and drink. Here is *vodki* in every imaginable kind of bottle. When people travel for months in temperatures below zero such elegant bottles must be very comforting."

Ten years later Smirnov received the official endorsement of Czar Alexander III, immediately changing the labels on his bottles to note the distinction. In 1893 Smirnov returned to America, this time to the Chicago World's Fair where, again, his bottles won honors. Smirnov ran ads not only touting his vodka's purity but also attacking counterfeit distillers. Supposedly he even launched a word-of-mouth campaign, in which paid individuals went into the city's bars and loudly demanded Smirnov vodka.

Five years later Smirnov died of a stroke. He was, at the time, one of the richest men in Russia, worth the equivalent of $132 million today. But between family infighting and the

< 18 >

Czar Alexander III, who endorsed Smirnov Vodka in 1886, by I. N. Kramskoi.

newly imposed imperial monopoly, it was only a matter of time before his empire started to crumble. Then came a series of calamities: the workers' strike of 1905, followed by outright prohibition in 1914, the catastrophic Great War, and the Bolshevik Revolution. Prohibition ended in 1925, but the Smirnov distillery now fell under the control of the Soviets, who targeted the Smirnov family for persecution.

Only one of Smirnov's sons, Vladimir, managed to escape the USSR. He eventually opened a small distillery in Paris under the company name Pierre Smirnoff Fils before moving down to Nice to settle within the Russian exile community there. Unfortunately, notes Himelstein, "his vodka business was sputtering—France was not taken by the taste of the colorless spirit, preferring its own wines and cognacs, nor did it seem that the rest of Europe had a thirst for vodka either." Smirnov should have moved to London, where vodka was gaining popularity. As one liquor wholesaler named Mrs. "Temperance" Fisher told the press in 1926: "I think there must be a large number of Russians in London because I sell so much vodka here. Englishmen are beginning to acquire a taste for it, too. Just at first it sometimes puts them under the table."

Nor was America clamoring for the spirit. Though Smirnov introduced his vodka to America in 1876 and again in 1893, it didn't catch on outside of ethnic enclaves. During the colonial era, the Triangular Trade—slaves from Africa to the Caribbean; sugar and molasses from the Caribbean to the American colonies; rum from the American colonies to Britain—transformed rum into the dominant spirit of the era. "By 1770," notes Wayne Curtis in *And a Bottle of Rum: A History of the New World in*

< 20 >

VOL. LVI   No. 1446.   PUCK BUILDING, New York, November 16, 1904.   PRICE TEN CENTS.

Copyright, 1904, by Keppler & Schwarzmann.

"What fools these Mortals be?"

Entered at N. Y. P. O. as Second-class Mail Matter.

RUNNING AMUCK.

A drunk, sword-wielding Russian by Udo J. Keppler, "Running Amuck," on the cover of *Puck* magazine (1904). *Courtesy of the Library of Congress*

Ten Cocktails, "the North American colonists were importing some 6.5 million gallons of molasses from the islands, which was distilled into about 5 million gallons of rum." According to some estimates, by the late 1700s, this amounted to five shots of rum per day for the average American over age fifteen.

But with the onset of taxes, embargoes, and the War of Independence, rum consumption declined. Curtis mentions Sam Adams, who ran the following advertisement: "It is to be hoped, that the Gentlemen of the Town will endeavor to bring our own October Beer into Fashion again, by that most prevailing Motive, Example, so that we may no longer be beholden to Foreigners for a Credible Liquor, which may be as successfully manufactured in this Country."

With an abundance of grain, the American farmer was more than willing to set the example. As Max Watman points out in *Chasing the White Dog: An Amateur Outlaw's Adventures in Moonshine:* "It's easier to transport grain that is stored as whiskey than it is to transport the raw product. Second, grain spoils, whiskey doesn't. Third, whiskey is always worth more than the grain that went into making it." By 1860, Watman writes, "the liquor business was booming. The nation produced almost 90 million gallons of spirits each year. Whiskey was cheap—24 cents a gallon in New York, 14 cents a gallon in Ohio—and none of it was taxed."

In 1862 publishing house Dick & Fitzgerald issued bartender Jerry Thomas's cocktail guide, *How to Mix Drinks, or The Bon Vivant's Companion,* the first book of its kind published in America. "We simply contend that a relish for 'social drinks' is universal," Thomas writes in the preface, "that those

< 22 >

HOW TO MIX DRINKS,

OR

THE BON-VIVANT'S COMPANION,

CONTAINING CLEAR AND RELIABLE DIRECTIONS FOR MIXING ALL THE BEVERAGES
USED IN THE UNITED STATES, TOGETHER WITH THE MOST POPULAR
BRITISH, FRENCH, GERMAN, ITALIAN, RUSSIAN, AND SPANISH
RECIPES, EMBRACING PUNCHES, JULEPS, COBBLERS,
ETC., ETC., ETC., IN ENDLESS VARIETY.

BY JERRY THOMAS,

Formerly principal Bar-tender at the Metropolitan Hotel, New York, and the Planter's House, St. Louis

TO WHICH IS APPENDED

A MANUAL FOR THE MANUFACTURE

OF

Cordials, Liquors, Fancy Syrups, &c., &c.,

AFTER THE MOST APPROVED METHODS NOW USED IN THE DISTILLATION OF
LIQUORS AND BEVERAGES, DESIGNED FOR THE SPECIAL USE OF
MANUFACTURERS AND DEALERS IN WINES AND SPIRITS,
GROCERS, TAVERN-KEEPERS, AND PRIVATE FAMI-
LIES, THE SAME BEING ADAPTED TO THE
TRADE OF THE UNITED STATES
AND CANADAS.

Illustrated with Descriptive Engravings.

THE WHOLE CONTAINING

OVER 600 VALUABLE RECIPES.

BY CHRISTIAN SCHULTZ,

Professor of Chemistry, Apothecary, and Manufacturer of Wines, Liquors, Cordials,
&c., &c., from Berne, Switzerland.

NEW YORK:

DICK & FITZGERALD, PUBLISHERS,

NO. 18 ANN STREET.

1862.

drinks exist in greater variety in the United States than in any other country in the world; and that he, therefore, who proposes to impart to these drinks not only the most palatable but the most wholesome characteristics of which they may be made susceptible, is a genuine public benefactor." Thomas, who had joined the Gold Rush at age nineteen, calls the

Albany wine cellar during Prohibition.
Courtesy of the Albany Library Historical Collection

< 24 >

cocktail "a modern invention, and is generally used on fishing and other sporting parties, although some patients insist that it is good in the morning as a tonic." The book contains 463 entries, including the Whiskey Cocktail, Gin Sour, and Crème de Nymphe, also known as a Lady's Cream. Not a single recipe contains vodka. Nevertheless, we have arrived at the dawn of the Golden Age of Drinking (a phrase coined by H. L. Mencken).

But just as in Russia, America faced a battle over alcohol, culminating in 1920 in the Eighteenth Amendment, making Prohibition the law of the land. It lasted thirteen years and failed miserably. Oklahoma's favorite son, laconic cowboy Will Rogers, famously said, "Prohibition is better than no liquor at all." Bootleggers thrived, and booze continued to flow—some of it lethal. When the Twenty-First Amendment finally reversed the ban, drinking culture had changed. "Serious imbibers who recalled the stylish cocktails served up prior to Prohibition were disheartened by unschooled hordes that filled the new bars to overflowing," writes Curtis. The new crowd "saw drink as a mere intoxicant rather than a centerpiece to a social ritual."

The stage was set.

3
BREATHLESS CHARM

When I started tending bar, nobody ever, ever ordered a vodka martini. Vodka martini? What is that? A martini is gin, olives. Very few people ordered vodka tonics. It was gin and tonic. It's like an invasive species.

—Michael Roper, owner of the
Hopleaf Bar, Chicago

Just as Prohibition was winding down, a New York business-man named Rudolph P. Kunett, born Kunettchenskiy in what is now Ukraine, got wind of Vladimir Smirnov's offer to license his vodka abroad. Kunett paid the distiller 54,000 francs in return for all the trademarks and exclusive rights. "If he could bring Smirnoff's beverages to the United States," writes Smirnov biographer Linda Himelstein, "he might be able to introduce the spirits to consumers, create demand for it, and make a fortune."

If only it were that easy. Kunett opened the Smirnoff distillery in March 1934 in Bethel, Connecticut. Vladimir died five months later without seeing the first vodka factory in

America. Of course there wasn't much to see: Kunett sold a mere 1,200 cases that first year.

Though sales steadily increased, Smirnoff was verging on bankruptcy until John Martin of G. F. Heublein & Bros. bought it from Kunett in 1938 for $14,000 ($226,500 today). Heublein itself wasn't in solid financial shape, depending largely on its A-1 steak sauce to get the company through hard times. But by the early 1940s, sales of Smirnoff had grown to more than twenty-two thousand cases a year. It helped that along the way several vodka-based cocktails had caught on.

First came the Bloody Mary, which initially consisted of vodka, tomato juice, Worcestershire sauce, salt, and pepper. Harry's New York Bar in Paris served it while America was still dry. But then Fernand Petiot, a bartender at Harry's, came to New York in 1934 and was hired by the St. Regis Hotel to work in the legendary King Cole Bar. When a customer named Serge Obolensky asked for a Bloody Mary, Petiot added lemon juice, cayenne pepper, and an olive garnish. It became the Red Snapper.

Sitting at the King Cole Bar beneath the Modernist mural of Old King Cole by Maxfield Parrish, Salim El Khayati, the hotel's senior food and beverage manager, discussed the name discrepancy. "We don't use the word 'Bloody Mary' in this hotel," he explains. "We use the Red Snapper—the St. Regis brand, you know, is always classy people, classy clients." It's red for the color, and "snapper" conveys the bite.

The Red Snapper became a huge hit, especially as a hangover cure, and even now it's the most requested drink at the hotel's bar. El Khayati estimates that bartenders make between twenty-eight and thirty-five Red Snappers each day,

< 28 >

Fernand Petiot, inventor of the Red Snapper (Bloody Mary) at the King Cole Bar inside the St. Regis Hotel, New York. *Courtesy of the St. Regis Hotel, New York*

The King Cole Bar at the St. Regis Hotel, New York.
Courtesy of the St. Regis Hotel, New York

though most customers call it a Bloody Mary. Either way, it'll set you back twenty dollars.

The Screwdriver, meanwhile, reportedly came about when American oil workers in the Middle East were discreetly pouring vodka in their orange juice, but, lacking a spoon, they stirred the drink with a screwdriver. Jon Taffer, host of Spike TV's *Bar Rescue,* loves telling the story of the Harvey Wallbanger, supposedly made by a Philadelphia bartender named Harvey. "It was a Screwdriver, vodka and orange juice, and he put Galliano on top. Galliano is an Italian liqueur, a very tall bottle. Because it's such a tall bottle, you can't leave it in the front. You gotta put it in the back because you can't reach the bottles behind

< 30 >

it. So every time he made the drink, he'd bang the wall, and his customers would say, 'Give me one of those wallbangers.'"

In 1941 John Martin of Heublein was at the Cock 'n' Bull, a British pub, on the Sunset Strip in Los Angeles. Bar owner Jack Morgan apparently was trying to promote his ginger beer when Martin suggested he mix it with Smirnoff vodka and a squeeze of lime. The result: the Moscow Mule. (Drinks writer Eric Felten disputes this claim, suggesting the Cock 'n' Bull's bartender more likely created it.) Served in a copper mug, the drink took off in Hollywood, then began to spread throughout the rest of California and across the country.

"For the first time an invented cocktail was being used as a marketing device," observes William Grimes in *Straight Up or On the Rocks: The Story of the American Cocktail.* "Heublein's salesmen traveled from bar to bar, explaining the drink to bar managers and supplying Moscow Mule signs to be displayed on walls and mirrors." Grimes suggests another reason for its popularity in Hollywood: "It allowed them [the film community] to drink on the set and elude the sharp eyes (and noses) of studio spies."

Indeed, vodka on the breath was discovered to be much less noticeable than any brown spirit or gin. "White whiskey, no taste, no smell," is how South Carolina wholesaler Ed Smith put it. Milton Goodman of the Lawrence Gumbinner ad agency refined this elegantly to "Smirnoff Leaves You

Old King Cole beholds a Red Snapper.
Courtesy of the St. Regis Hotel, New York

< 33 >

Breathless," resulting in a campaign packed with endorsements from celebrities, including Woody Allen, Zsa Zsa Gabor, Eartha Kitt, Buster Keaton, and Groucho Marx. (Another ad campaign, known as "Driest of the Dry," featured a photo by Bert Stern of a martini glass and the Great Pyramid of Giza in the background, with the pyramid upside down in the drink.)

One ad showing Woody Allen on a beach literally coming out of his shell reads:

> *Everyone else is enjoying these Smirnoff drinks. Why not you? Smirnoff Screwdrivers with orange juice, Smirnoff Bloody Marys with tomato juice, Smirnoff Mules made with 7-Up. The dryest Martinis. The smoothest drink on the rocks. Only Smirnoff, filtered through 11,000 pounds of activated charcoal, makes so many drinks so well. Come out where the sun and the Smirnoff shine. It's a delicious world! Always ask for Smirnoff Vodka. It leaves you breathless.*

In the 1958 edition of *The Fine Art of Mixing Drinks,* cocktail historian David Embury notes:

> *In the last half of 1950, the first period for which figures were published by the federal government, there were less*

"Production. Industrial alcohol. In the 'high wine' room of a former whiskey distillery, high-test ethyl alcohol (190 proof) is produced for the making of explosives. Fifteen huge copper tanks are used for the storage, proofing and gauging of the alcohol." Photo, circa 1942 (during World War II) by Howard Liberman. *Courtesy of the Library of Congress*

< 35 >

Eartha Kitt muling for the camera in a 1966 Smirnoff ad.

Courtesy of Diageo PLC

A Moscow Mule properly served.
Photo by Edsel Little

than 387,000 gallons of vodka bottled in the United States. For the year 1955, the figure jumped to almost seven million gallons. Of this amount, well over one third was sold on the Pacific coast and Heublein alone sold over 40 per cent of the total.

That same year, *Time* magazine reported that "nonwhisky liquors have . . . bounced up, nearly doubling their market share since 1949 to 23 percent. The reason again is mildness: odorless, light-bodied vodka has jumped from virtually nothing to 6 percent of liquor sales."

Relating an interesting countermove to the supposed subtlety of vodka breath, Daniel Oliver, a former chairman of the Federal Trade Commission in the Reagan administration, says that the partners at his old law firm advised him to drink brown spirits as opposed to vodka: "That way the client will know you're drunk and not just acting stupid."

Then we have the matter of a certain member of the British Secret Service. In 1953 in Ian Fleming's first James Bond novel, *Casino Royale,* the dark and brooding Agent 007 doesn't at first drink a vodka martini, shaken or stirred. No, his first alcoholic beverage is a whiskey on the rocks. But soon after he asks a bartender for a dry martini "in a deep champagne goblet." But he was only getting started: "Just a moment. Three measures of Gordon's, one of vodka, half a measure of Kina Lillet. Shake it very well until it's ice cold, then add a large thin slice of lemon-peel. Got it?" Bond names it the Vesper, after his counterpart, Vesper Lynd.

But in 1962 when *Dr. No,* the first canonical Bond movie, was released, 007 clearly drinks a vodka martini, shaken, not

< 38 >

stirred, provided by his eponymous villain, and the brand was Smirnoff. According to Roger Moore in *Bond on Bond: Reflections on 50 Years of James Bond Movies:* "This fleeting moment in the film literally changed the way Martini drinkers made their cocktails from then on, shifting from the traditional gin to a vodka-based drink and popularizing the vodka Martini the world over." Moore himself prefers a gin martini, proper, though.

> *My gin of choice is Tanqueray, and the vermouth has to be Noilly Prat. Take the glass or cocktail shaker you are using, and, for two sensible-sized Martinis, fill ¼ of each glass with Noilly Prat. Swill it around and then discard it. Next, top the glasses up with gin, drop in a zest of lemon, and place the glasses in a freezer or ice-cold fridge until you are—or should I say she is—ready.*

In 1967 vodka had overtaken gin as the most popular white spirit in the country. The following year, Donald Kendall, the chairman of Pepsi, flew to Moscow and worked out a deal, allowing the soda to be sold in the Soviet Union in return for Stolichnaya Vodka, over which Pepsi obtained distribution rights. It was the first Russian vodka sold in America.

By 1976 vodka had surpassed gin and whiskey as the nation's most dominant spirit—this despite the poor quality of most brands, the vast majority of which were American. Michael Roper, owner of the Hopleaf Bar in Chicago, remembers one brand in particular, called Mohawk, which he describes as "cheap, cheap, cheap. Mohawk had a factory just outside Detroit along the expressway and . . . all

< 39 >

Cocktail bar and restaurant at Hunts Point Market in the Bronx, New York City, 1967, by Nat Fein. *Courtesy of the New York* World-Telegram *and the* Sun *Newspaper Photograph Collection, Library of Congress*

their products were made there. It's almost like they turned a switch—whiskey, vodka, gin—and it was all junk." He adds, "When I started tending bar, every vodka brand had to have a Russian eagle. . . . You had to have some name that made you think they were from Russia, 'by appointment to the czar' or something. But they were very, very harsh."

Even Smirnoff, still the most popular vodka brand on the market in the 1970s, had lost some of its shine. "I remember years ago when Smirnoff was a dirty word," Jon Taffer recalls. "Smirnoff, we used to say, 'They get the water from the Detroit River.' It was a dirty name. It was cheap. It was terrible." That said, Taffer points out, "Smirnoff is the greatest success story in the history of vodka. They took this garbage brand—garbage—and they reinvented it, won taste tests all

< 40 >

over America, turned it into a premier brand, made it proud, gave it a big chest. It's an unbelievable story of brand management and brand reinvention."

So what accounts for the spirit's popularity?

"Cheap availability—that's the really big thing," says John Jeffery, master distiller at Death's Door distillery in Wisconsin. "The technology that developed around the ethanol-fuel industry is really what made it possible to bulk produce vodka cheaply. That technology, which is derived from petroleum cracking columns, evolved with Big Oil. . . . As an alternative to Big Oil, Big Corn created these ethanol plants, and these ethanol plants are really the derivation of the huge, continuous stills that produce modern, extremely neutral, bulk spirits. Before the widely available tall, continuous column, there's no way that vodka was as neutral as it is today."

This development, after World War II, coincides with the federal government's decree in 1949 of the definition of vodka as "neutral spirits distilled from any material at or above 190 proof, reduced to not more than 110 proof and not less than 80 proof, and, after such reduction in proof, so treated as to be without distinctive character, aroma, or taste." Jeffery suggests this definition intentionally favored the giant distillers; only they had the capacity to fulfill these guidelines.

Plus, cultural considerations came into play. "Think about the 1970s," says DC mixologist Derek Brown. "You don't drink an Old-Fashioned if your dad drank an Old-Fashioned because you're a hippy and hippies don't—you can't see a hippy going, 'I'll take an Old-Fashioned.' It just doesn't even make sense."

< 41 >

Lance Winters of St. George Spirits sees a combination of factors: "the power of marketing, the sexiness of the martini but the unwillingness for people to go with something that's very full flavored, and whiskey, which is more for old men in boardrooms. . . . It was sexy to drink a vodka martini. It was something that was going to be less apparent on your breath than a lot of other spirits. It was something you could hide with a bunch of other ingredients." He points out, as others have, that "we didn't drink for a long time to enjoy a good quality spirit. We drank to be anesthetized. As Americans, we like all of our bitter pills to have a candy coating on the outside. Vodka was very easy to candy-coat. . . . It was a chameleon. A lot of other spirits, you can't say that about."

"Women became more sophisticated," says Roper. "They also started ordering their own drinks. . . . When women moved up through the business world and became more independent in all their decisions, they said, 'You know, I don't really like all that sugary crap.' I want to order the same kinds of things for the same kinds of reasons that men do."

And sugary crap it was. Take, for instance, the Pink Lady: one egg white, one teaspoon grenadine, one teaspoon sweet cream, one-and-a-half ounces gin. Or the Lady Alexander (as opposed to the Brandy Alexander), comprising equal parts crème de cacao and sloe gin, one egg white, and a dash of Angostura bitters.

"When I started tending bar," Roper recalls, "there was like a women's ghetto on the drink list, and if they drank spirits at all, it was always something where there was so much fruit and sugar and other stuff and spritz to cover up the flavor of whiskey or the liquor—it didn't matter what it was.

< 42 >

You couldn't tell whether there was whiskey, gin, or vodka in the thing."

"I think vodka was originally more of a less challenging flavor than"—Roper stops himself, knowing he's stepped on a landmine of political correctitude. "Oh women are going to like that," he adds with a laugh. But, he continues, "They're not going to like Scotch; that's for cigar-smoking burly men. The same with Kentucky whiskey. It was unladylike to drink Kentucky whiskey, but it was considered somewhat ladylike to have a fancy cocktail with an olive in it."

But couldn't producers find a better vodka to put in that fancy cocktail?

Absolutely.

< 43 >

4
ABSOLUT POWER

One—there's no market. Two—I'm not into vodka. And three—the bottle looks like shit. Forget it.
—Al Singer, Carillon Importers, in Carl Hamilton's *Absolut: Biography of a Bottle*

In the opening to a *Simpsons* episode that aired in November 2011, two publicists approach Krusty the Clown with a problem. "We're having trouble persuading people it's hip to drink a vodka made by a clown in a bottle shaped like a clown that does this when you open it," one of them says, then removes the cap. A vintage car horn blares.

"Plus, that TV special where you drank another brand of vodka didn't help," says the other.

"I used up my stuff poisoning deer," says Krusty.

The solution? "If we're ever going to sell your vodka, we need to do something completely unorthodox—a viral marketing campaign. . . . People are more likely to drink your vodka if they think all their coolest friends are drinking it, so we pay for a big party at the home of a Springfield trendsetter. . . .

< 45 >

He invites his cool friends. We serve free cocktails made with your vodka, generating buzz."

The party—at the Simpsons' house, of course—is a smashing success. From two spouts in the nostrils, a giant Krusty head dispenses vodka martinis. The name of the vodka is Absolut Krusty.

Pernod Ricard, corporate owner of Absolut Vodka, would no doubt have preferred something less cynical, and of course they had nothing to do with the episode. But being parodied on the longest-running sitcom in television history says something. Absolut had become a cultural icon.

When the American Marketing Association inducted Absolut into its Hall of Fame in 1992, the vodka producer joined the ranks of just two other inductees: Coca-Cola and Nike, both of which had the advantage of television. Since liquor commercials were illegal at the time, Absolut relied strictly on print. If you went to college in the 1980s or 1990s, you probably remember those Absolut ads plastered all over dorm room walls.

In July 2002 *Forbes* ranked Absolut as the top-rated luxury brand in the world over the likes of Tiffany, the Ritz-Carlton, and BMW. The next highest ranking liquor was Bacardi in tenth place. It comes as no surprise, then, that the executives at Pernod Ricard refer to it as one of their two "global iconic brands."[2]

---

2 The other is Chivas Regal. That's right, the blended Scotch whiskey of your father's and grandfather's generation remains *that* popular in America. The land of the free is still the second-best market for the brand. The top market? The People's Republic of China.

< 46 >

It almost didn't happen.

Today a marketable vodka can come from anywhere: Iceland, Idaho, France, Texas. But in 1978, trying to convince American importers to carry a vodka from Sweden of all places was no easy task. Virtually all vodka consumed in the United States was domestic: Georgi, Kamchatka, Mohawk, Popov, Smirnoff (of course), and Wolfschmidt. The only actual foreign brands—as opposed to brands with foreign-sounding names—were Stolichnaya from the Soviet Union, Wyborowa from Poland, and Finlandia from Finland.

So why did the sneaky Swedes think they could sell their vodka in America? They'd been drinking the neutral grain spirit since 1467, sure, but Americans didn't know that. In 1978 vodka wasn't the first thing that came to mind when you thought of Sweden. ABBA, meatballs, and maybe Björn Borg, who won Wimbledon and the French Open that year. But that was about it. Vin & Sprit, a government entity, had controlled Swedish vodka, known as Absolut Rent Brännvin or Renat to the Swedes, since 1917. The state strictly regulated alcohol production and consumption. Until 1955, all Swedish citizens (twenty-five years and older) had to possess a liquor ration book to purchase alcohol of any kind. The whole system was notoriously oppressive.

Author Carl Hamilton describes the insanity: "If you were holding a party, you were permitted to buy more than your standard allowance. So the Control Agency ordered the liquor stores to inform them of every party taking place in the whole country. Every one. With all the details. Fiftieth birthdays, wedding receptions, office parties, who was there, and how much did they drink?" For anyone who liked to imbibe—and there's not a whole lot else to do during those long, dark Swedish winters—it was like living in East Germany:

> *Nationwide registers were compiled listing the names of alcoholics and those at risk of becoming alcoholics. People's marital status was recorded, along with information about their place of residence, income, and tax details. Misbehavior could result in a note in the register, and much prized information was gathered about suspect individuals in small towns by asking their neighbors.*

But the government viewed profits from alcohol as unseemly. Increases in revenue went hand in hand with higher taxes to deter citizens from drinking more. When the subject of selling the whole Absolut Rent Brännvin operation abroad came up, rather than "poisoning" the native population further, one executive asked if his fellow countrymen were prepared to "export sin."

But decide they did. Studies showed that Americans had developed a liking for the clear spirit, which now surpassed gin and whiskey in terms of consumption. If Americans *wanted* to spend their dollars on Swedish vodka, profits could flow guiltlessly back to the coffers of the kingdom of Sweden, and the state could use all that money to bolster its very comfortable welfare system.

Americans, however, remained skeptical.

All the major importers—Austin Nichols, Brown-Forman, Heublein, Hiram Walker, Paddington, and Seagram—shot down Vin & Sprit's president Lars Lindmark and Curt Nycander, director of export. Heublein, which made Smirnoff, had the audacity

< 48 >

to ask the Swedes if they wanted to consider distilling Russian grain into spirits for sale in America. Hamilton quotes veteran advertising executive Marvin Shankman as saying, "As far as I know, the world doesn't need a new vodka. Especially not a Swedish vodka. And especially not one that you can't see."

Especially not one that you can't see. That was the oddest part of the pitch. The Swedish vodka came in what looked like a medicine bottle. The neck was short, making it difficult for bartenders to handle, and the printing was etched onto the glass itself. You could look straight through it and see the brand on the shelf behind it. According to Carl Hamilton, liquor consultant Joe Tomassi advised the Swedes to be bold: "A vodka bottle must stand tall. It should have a large red label, a number of royal crowns, lions, and unicorns, and preferably a Russian name."

When New York ad firm N. W. Ayer took a first look at it, in-house reactions included "What the hell is this?" "That bottle, it's like East Berlin. It's un-American," and "To me this looks like a bottle of antifreeze." These observations came from one of the most venerable agencies in the country, which had thought up "When it rains it pours" for Morton's salt, "Reach out and touch someone" for AT&T, and "Be all that you can be" for the US Army. N. W. Ayer knew what it was doing.

But the Swedes pressed. Anyway, the alternatives looked dreadful. Hamilton mentions one prototype involving "a wild man, with flowing blond locks and a beard, sword swinging from his side . . . standing between two female partygoers wearing cocktail dresses. They held martini glasses in their hands, and one stood charmed by an olive stuck on the end of a toothpick." They considered alternate names, such as

< 49 >

Royal Court Vodka, Blonde Swede, and Damn Swede. Seeing these contenders now is like learning that Danny Thomas and Ernest Borgnine were considered for the role of Vito Corleone in *The Godfather*.[3]

In the end, one tiny distributor—Carillon Importers of New York, purveyors of the better known Bombay Gin and Grand Marnier—decided to take a chance. But even then, it was no sure thing. Al Singer, Carillon's head, explicitly said, "I don't want a vodka." Hamilton quotes him going even further: "One—there's no market. Two—I'm not into vodka. And three—the bottle looks like shit. Forget it." But a few trips to Absolut's home in the village of Åhus in Sweden, along with his then-advertising counterpart, Martin Landey of Martin Landey Arlow, convinced Singer to give it a go.

But first they had to make a few tweaks to the bottle design, including the addition of a medallion bearing the image of Lars Olsson Smith, the Swedish inventor who in 1879 developed the rectification process, which removed more impurities than ever before. The end result was Absolut Rent Brännvin, described thus: "This superb vodka was distilled from grain grown in the rich fields of southern Sweden. It has been produced at the famous old distilleries near Åhus in accordance with more than 400 years of Swedish tradition. Vodka has been sold under the name Absolut since 1879."

Note the subtlety of the phrase "in accordance with more than 400 years of Swedish tradition." Absolut hasn't sat on

---

3 It's true.

< 50 >

liquor shelves for the last four centuries, but the description cleverly makes you think that it has. As any ad executive will tell you, an enduring history lures consumers. (As we will see, this selling point was not lost on Ketel One, which does come from a distillery operated by the same family in the same location since 1691, though the initial products were primarily jenevers, gins, and bitters.)

Absolut finally made its American debut in 1979 at the Fairmont Hotel in New Orleans. Sales were unremarkable. One of the few places that kept ordering cases of Absolut on a consistent basis turned out to be a gay bar in Boston. In a few years' time, Absolut's connection to the gay community grew far more profound, but for now it was slower going. At the end of 1980, eleven thousand cases had been sold.

Word of mouth certainly helped. Another Swede, Peter Ekelund of Vin and Sprit, went from bar to bar in Manhattan introducing the new vodka to New Yorkers.[4] But advertising proved problematic.

To begin, the Swedes didn't really know how to advertise alcohol, which for many years was largely outlawed in their country and allowed only on matchboxes. Second, just as Absolut was rolling out, Carillon Importers went looking for a new advertising agency. In a *Mad Men*–style twist, another agency, Geers Gross, took over Martin Landey Arlow. One of the Geers Gross clients was liquor giant Brown Forman, which sparked a conflict of interest. Geers Gross relinquished

---

4 Ekelund later cofounded Swedish rival Karlsson's Gold.

< 51 >

VODKA

the Carillon account. Some ninety-four other agencies fought for it, including one called TBWA.

It doesn't exactly roll off the tongue—TBWA. It didn't get any easier when it later became TBWA\Chiat\Day.[5] Still, it was better than having to say Tragos, Bonnange, Wiesendanger, Ajroldi, Chiat, Day each time. But the firm had a stable of extraordinary talent. Those unwieldy names had all worked at the legendary firm Young and Rubicam. Y&R had created the first research department, under George Gallup, for an ad agency and ran the first "demo" ad as well as the first color commercial on television, for Jell-O.

During the bidding over the Carillon account in the fall of 1980, Geoff Hayes, TBWA's art director, was sketching Absolut bottles while watching *The Honeymooners.* In a moment of silliness, he drew a halo atop the vodka and wrote, "Absolut. It's the perfect vodka." That levity proved key to the future of the brand.

The next day, writer Graham Turner suggested they shorten the tagline to "Absolut Perfection." In *Absolut Book: The Absolut Vodka Advertising Story,* Richard W. Lewis explains that

---

5 Yes, back slashes. Really.

The first of many ads that transformed Absolut Vodka into an icon.
© *The Absolut Company AB*

< 52 >

ABSOLUT PERFECTION.

together they turned out a few more ads, and soon a format emerged: In just two words (the first one always being Absolut*), the ad would say something complimentary or flattering about either the product itself or the person drinking it, and, importantly, add a dollop of humor so the "We're the best" claim wouldn't be quite so boring or pretentious.*

According to Lewis, the challenge was that

they had to establish that Absolut was the best vodka on the market, without actually saying that in an ad. That kind of advertising claim—"This is the best [whatever] that money can buy"—is both boring and unpersuasive. (In fact, you stand a better chance of convincing consumers that you really have a great product if you display a little modesty and let them discover it for themselves. Consumers are continually assaulted by advertisers' superiority claims, and are thus not unreasonably skeptical.)

The ads persuaded Carillon to go with TBWA.

Yet that original ad, "Absolut Perfection," soon became a disaster. The clear bottle presented a challenge. When combined with conventional lighting techniques, the vodka looked more like milk and the overall ad cartoonish. Hayes turned to

---

One of the early Absolut ads, making very clear this vodka is from Sweden.
© *The Absolut Company AB*

< 54 >

ABSOLUT CLARITY.

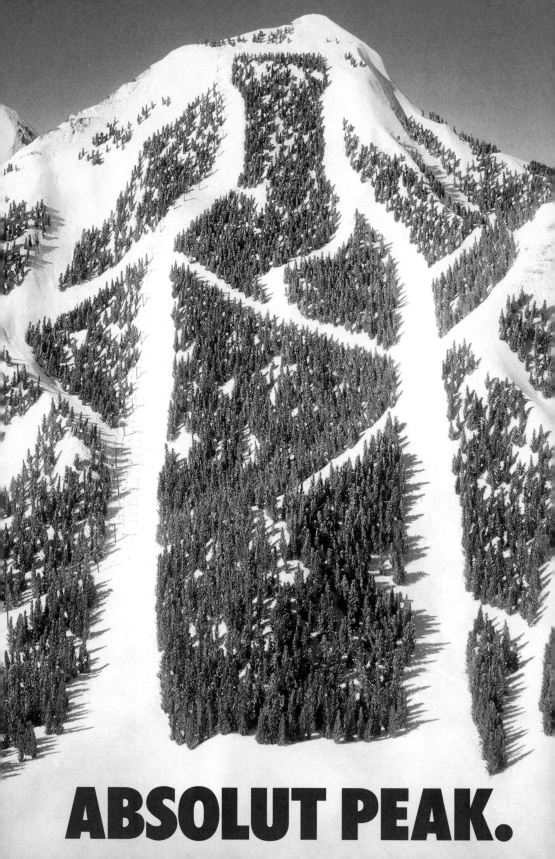

ABSOLUT PEAK.

photographer Steve Bronstein, who tried something different: using a ton of reflectors and shooting the bottle in front of a matte Plexiglas sheet, giving it the soft glow now familiar to us all.

The follow-up ad, "Absolut Clarity," had more to it than just a magnifying glass. Lewis, who became TBWA's worldwide account manager for the vodka, observes, "At a time when the Soviet Union was particularly unpopular in the United States due to its invasion of Afghanistan and, later, the downing of a Korean jetliner, this ad subtly emphasized the fact that Absolut was made in Sweden, not in Russia." Then came the rest: "Absolut Attraction" (martini glass bending toward the bottle), "Absolut Bravo" (red roses strewn about it), "Absolut Treasure" (bottle in an aquarium), "Absolut Joy" (the bottle dressed up like a Christmas tree), and "Absolut Larceny" (a broken chain and lock—significant because the underlying assumption was that the brand was becoming widely recognized).

By the mid-1980s some expressed concern the ad campaign was running out of steam—or at the very least, descriptives. (Hayes and Turner came up with most of them.) But then came "Absolut Stardom," in which a series of lightbulbs represented the shape of the bottle, as if it were a Broadway marquee. This innovation opened the door to a whole other series of ads, such as "Absolut Peak" (downhill ski slopes in

Not just anything could represent the bottle. There had to be status, a statement about lifestyle. Here, it's skiing. © *The Absolut Company AB*

< 57 >

the shape of the bottle) and the golf-themed "Absolut 19th." Anything resembling it could now replace the bottle. Well, not *anything*: "They had to possess or reflect either a high value, such as gold, or an upscale activity, such as skiing or golf," says Lewis. "It may not have been obvious to the reader, but we perennially strove to build upon Absolut's premium image."

When Absolut targeted the California market in 1988, it came out with "Absolut L.A." (a swimming pool shaped like the bottle). If you're doing Los Angeles, you had better do New York City, too—"Absolut Manhattan" showed a satellite image of the island with Central Park resembling the bottle. Soon, cities across the country and around the world became Absolut ads, each cleverly depicted and gloriously shot. The wind blows away the words on the bottle for "Absolut Chicago." "Absolut Miami" depicts an extremely detailed model of an art deco hotel, and "Absolut D.C." fittingly showed the bottle wrapped in red tape. (An amusing section in *Absolut Book* features rejected ads, including "Absolut Memphis"—an Elvis sideburn resembling the bottle—and "Absolut Philadelphia"—the ad itself torn in the middle like the Liberty Bell, which the creatives deemed too obvious.)

Still, it wasn't enough for Michel Roux, who succeeded Al Singer at Carillon. Roux explored other ways to further the brand, particularly in the worlds of art and fashion. In 1985 he

The glass bottle itself was no longer needed—the possibilities for this campaign were practically endless. © *The Absolut Company AB*

< 58 >

ABSOLUT STARDOM.

paid Andy Warhol $65,000 for his own rendition of the vodka, "Absolut Warhol." That commission led to "Absolut Basquiat," "Absolut Haring," "Absolut Hirschfeld," "Absolut Neiman," and many more artists. The brand sponsored a series of men's fashions in *GQ* and women's in *Vogue, Elle,* and elsewhere. It also became actively involved in other causes and campaigns, such as AIDS research and gay rights.

Meanwhile, business was booming. Sales in America jumped from 11,000 cases in 1980 to 444,000 cases in 1984. In 1989 it surpassed Stolichnaya as the number one imported vodka in America—rather fitting considering the fall of the Eastern Bloc that year and the demise of the Soviet Union two years later.

In 1994 Absolut's parent owner, Vin & Sprit, named Seagram its worldwide distributor. TBWA remained the ad agency of record, but Carillon was out of luck as importer. Carillon did pick up another vodka to distribute, Stolichnaya, but this proved short lived. Stoli changed hands again, ultimately landing at William Grant & Sons. Michel Roux later quit the company and started the not-so-subtly-named Crillon, which has a decent stable of brands, including Rhum Barbancourt, but nothing quite like Absolut.

In 2008 Pernod Ricard, owner of Beefeater Gin, Chivas Regal, Glenlivet Scotch, and Jameson Irish Whiskey, among other brands, purchased Absolut from the kingdom of Sweden

Absolut was not just about vodka. It was about art.
©1985 The Andy Warhol Foundation for the Visual Arts, © The Absolut Company AB

< 61 >

for $8.3 billion. Six banks had to finance the loan, which was expected to take four years for a return on investment.

Despite the vodka boom of the late 1990s and the thousand or so competitors that have flooded the market, Americans still consume five million cases' worth of Absolut each year. Total annual volume sits roughly at ten million cases. It is available in 126 countries and comes in nineteen varieties, such as Berri Açai, Cilantro, Hibiskus, and Orient Apple—but not Absolut Krusty.

< 62 >

5

THE DUTCH MASTERS

Jerry: Holland is the Netherlands.
George: Then who are the Dutch?

—*SEINFELD*, SEASON 9, EPISODE 1

Just as Absolut was preparing to take America by storm, a Dutch distiller named Carolus Nolet was contemplating something similar. In the 1970s vodka had just overtaken whiskey, bourbon, and gin as the nation's most popular spirit. But would Americans want vodka from Holland?

In retrospect the answer is obvious. We as a country have warmly embraced Mr. Nolet's Ketel One. It may trail Absolut and Grey Goose, but Ketel ships more than two million cases to the United States each year. It's the fourth most-preferred brand according to a 2012 survey (top three: Grey Goose, Absolut, Smirnoff). The commercials sound the heavy bass guitar riff from the opening of Black Rebel Motorcycle Club's "Spread Your Love," and in one of them, young, good-looking masters of the universe celebrate some billion-dollar deal, over which comes the voiceover:

< 63 >

There was a time when substance was style, when men were unmoved by the constant current of the crowd, when they didn't drink their vodka from delicately painted perfume bottles. There was a time when men were men. It was last night. Inspired by three hundred years of tradition, Ketel One. Gentlemen, this is vodka.

There's that word again: tradition. Three centuries of it, too. But how inspired are we talking? As it turns out, they make the vodka in the same distillery where they've produced spirits since 1691. It's a family business, eleven generations all told.

The Nolet Distillery lies in the port city of Schiedam, near Rotterdam, in South Holland, a province that considers itself more industrious than its northern neighbor. A saying in these parts goes: "What Rotterdam earns, Amsterdam burns." One retired Dutchman explained it thus: "The government takes all the tax money from the south and gives it to the north."[6] Schiedam has always been known for distilling. It has a distillation museum (as well as a museum dedicated to the exciting

---

6 The mutual animosity runs even deeper in the world of sports. Rotterdam's Feyenoord soccer team and Amsterdam's Ajax have declared themselves mutual enemies. Their matches, known as *de klassieker,* feature so much hooliganism that for the last few years fans of the visiting team have been banned from matches.

The Nolet Distillery and windmill. *Courtesy of the Nolet Distillery*

< 64 >

world of grinding corn by windmill). Some four hundred distilleries dotted the city in the late nineteenth century. They churned out jenever, Holland's official spirit from which gin had evolved in the seventeenth century—not coincidentally the height of Dutch international power. On the flavor scale, jenever lies somewhere between vodka and gin. Add drops of malt wine and gin to your vodka, and you basically have jenever.

During World War II, the Germans hit Schiedam's ports along the Nieuwe Maas River and flattened neighboring Rotterdam. It took the Nazi war machine just five days to conquer the tiny kingdom. The Allies then bombarded Schiedam's German-controlled shipyards as the tides of the war turned. After the war, forty distilleries were still operating, but one by one—partly because of technological advances and also consolidation—they closed up shop. Except, of course, for Nolet.

Inge Timmermans, Nolet's soft-spoken head of hospitality, comes down a flight of stairs to the sleek, postmodern lobby. She looks like Lois Maxwell, the actress who played Moneypenny in the Bond movies. She leads me on a brief tour through the distillery—no photos, please—including the bottling and packaging areas, eventually arriving at a cafe where we eagerly await a member of the Nolet dynasty. The litany of distillers begins with Joannes in 1691. The lineage of his successors, all Nolets, goes as follows: Jacobus, Joannes, Joannes, Jacobus, Joannes, Jacobus, Joannes, Paulus, Carolus, and his sons Carl Jr. and Bob.

At seventy-two, Carolus helms the enterprise. One of his sons, Carl, serves as executive vice president of Nolet Spirits USA and lives with his family in California. Bob is the executive vice president of the Nolet Distillery and lives in Schiedam,

< 66 >

The Nolet Dynasty: sons Carl Jr. (left) and Bob flank their father Carolus.
Courtesy of the Nolet Distillery

just down the street. A tall fellow—like most Dutch people, statistically the tallest in the world—he's in his forties, married with two sons, and quite possibly the last man still sporting a Mike Brady perm.

He attended the University of California at Irvine, although he may have learned more about Asia than America.[7] Looking back, he counts it an advantage because it helped him understand the cultural sensitivies among the Chinese, Koreans, and Japanese. "We didn't know. We have Germany from World War II," and that was it.

---

7 A 2012 UC Irvine freshman enrollment report breaks down the demographics: Asians, 55.7 percent, followed by Caucasians, 17.5 percent.

< 67 >

Inge and distillery ambassador Dennis Tamse join us for coffee and delicate *koekjes.* Tamse had just flown in from Panama where he was providing "spirits education" to other bartenders. The Nolets send their staff around the globe to make sure Ketel is used properly and not collecting dust on a shelf. It's part of a deliberate strategy by Carolus Nolet to ensure Ketel's continuing place in the world.

When Carolus took over for his father, Paulus, the distillery was still making a wide range of products: jenevers, gins, liqueurs, and bitters. But rather than sell a large amount of middling brands, Carolus decided to focus on one product only—jenever—and make it the best. Before long, Nolet's Ketel 1 Jenever became not only the top-selling brand in the Netherlands but also more expensive than the rest. It achieved the best of both worlds. On that solid foundation Carolus reconsidered exporting, since 90 percent of the distillery's production traditionally had gone abroad.

The United States looked like an alluring market. Vodka had become its number one spirit—something that could be made virtually overnight and from anywhere. It didn't need aging in barrels or to come from a particular region known for its *terroir.* Only a handful of imported vodkas had infiltrated the American market in the late 1970s and early 1980s: Absolut, Stolichnaya, Wyborowa, and Finlandia. Carolus Nolet saw room for one more.

But as it turns out, the company had done business in America before. Carolus's grandfather, Joannes Nolet—the fourth and final Joannes on the list above—operated a distillery in Baltimore that sold spirits at the turn of the twentieth century. Framed on a wall hangs a sales sheet from 1902

< 68 >

The Romanov coat of arms.

that records a case of gin as costing $7.25. The distillery also has a promotional piece for Imperial Eagle Vodka: "Distilled from Grain in the 'Moscow' Buildings by Distilleries J. A. J. Nolet, Schiedam-Holland, Est. 1691." The undated ad touts the brand's attributes—"with no after breath at all"—and its

< 69 >

purpose as the "ideal base for cocktails." For a time the Nolets owned the commercial trademark for the Romanov family's double-eagle crest. It's even painted on a wall.

It all came to an unfortunate end with Prohibition. Says Bob, "My father looked at the stories but was told 'We don't talk about that anymore because he [Joannes] had to flee the country basically and lost so much money in the United States.' It wasn't a very good story to tell." Then came an opportunity to tell a better story.

Carolus methodically spent seven years developing the right vodka for the American market. First he told his neutral grain spirit supplier, about two hours away by car, that "you need to go into a new quality." Carolus wanted a better cut of wheat to make ultra-wheat spirits sold exclusively to Nolet. He got what he wanted, making Ketel One's Nolet's neutral grain spirits vastly superior, Bob insists.

At the distillery, this ultra-wheat spirit runs through a series of column stills and copper pot stills, including the oldest coal-fired pot still at the facility, Distilleerketel No. 1—whence: Ketel One. The distillates then go into a master pot-still batch for blending, the way reserve wine is used to balance non-vintage wines to maintain consistency of fla-vor. Nearby, a bunker houses a million-liter tank of reserve Ketel One used for this master pot-still blend. The bottles are washed out with Ketel One and then filled with Ketel One.

In addition to being meticulous, Carolus is also a bit of a contrarian. "He always felt in himself, 'If I do something, I want to make it different—different than anybody else,'" says Bob. "Introducing a new product you already have no chance, but, if you're making something the same as what's already

< 70 >

out there, then you even have less than zero chance." This reasoning explains why Carolus decided in 1983 to launch Ketel One not in New York but rather in San Francisco, specifically at the BIX Restaurant and Supper Club in Jackson Square.

"The owner was behind the bar, he [Carolus] sat down, and asked what kind of vodka was his preference," recalls Bob. "The owner had a certain vodka and said, 'Oh, this is the best vodka!' He was really being an American, he was convinced." Carolus then asked, "Maybe you want to taste it room temperature next to this [Ketel One] if you want to see any differences between our vodka and what you think is the best?" Sure enough, the owner described Ketel One as "'a lot nicer to drink,' and he started to sell Ketel One for us to everybody who came in. It was his vodka."

Encouraging bartenders and distributors to do the selling formed part of Ketel One's strategy. But it also meant that each establishment that wanted to carry Ketel One had to meet with Nolet's team. Bob remembers when a wholesaler said,

Ketel One.
Courtesy of the Nolet Distillery

< 71 >

The Ketel One potstill.
Courtesy of the Nolet Distillery

"Okay, this bar wants to order Ketel One. What do we do?" Carolus instructed the wholesaler not to deliver anything. "We'll go there and explain to them that, if they want to have Ketel One, we need to do tastings, we need to do seminars, we need to explain the product. Otherwise there is no reason to sell it to them because it will end up on the back bar, and nobody will use it." In the beginning the Nolet distillery wouldn't sell Ketel by the case, selling only a smattering of bottles that first year. They also priced it five dollars higher than Absolut, making it the most expensive vodka on the market at the time.

But from BIX, where bartenders hung out after hours, Ketel One spread throughout the City by the Bay, becoming a bartender favorite. The head of Young's Market, a major distributor in California, noticed the brand's sudden popularity and approached Nolet about doing business. "Basically we said every bar needs education, all these things that are really important for Ketel One," Bob explains. "So step by step, one bar at a time . . . that's how we got from San Francisco and turned it into California, and from California we were discovered by all the other wholesalers."

In 2008 the Nolets agreed to sell a 50 percent stake in Ketel One to liquor giant Diageo, in exchange for global distribution. Bob calls it a win-win situation. Ivan Menezes, Diageo's CEO, carefully pitched the deal. "It's not like he came here and said, 'We'd like to buy you,'" according to Bob. "He said, 'We know you're a family business. You've been around for eleven generations. We want to continue that.' It's not somebody who says, 'Here, have money, you buy a boat, and we take over.' No—because this is what we do. This is our

< 73 >

blood. My children will hopefully want to do that. We got distribution around the world. I go to the Philippines, the product is there. I don't have to worry about getting it there."[8] Diageo made them an offer they couldn't refuse: For that 50 percent stake and worldwide distribution, the Nolets received $900 million.

The money shows. Robotics does most of the moving of cases and pallets; few forklifts are driven around. A canal that flows into the Nieuwe Maas River divides the distillery, so in the past transporting bottles back and forth involved a circuitous route, plus time and money lost. So the Nolets built a tunnel underneath the canal, the entire length of which a conveyor belt runs. It's the only private tunnel in the country.

We had coffee in a cafe inside a windmill built in 2005. The building's slanted elevator can take you to the top-floor observatory or down to the movie theater, which shows promotional videos: The first, a slick intro to Ketel One, will make your mouth water. The second is a fifteen-minute featurette called *A Timeless Mystery* from acclaimed Dutch director Pieter Rim de Kroon. It's a frenetically paced, time-jumping film that acts [as] an extended commercial for Nolet Gin. The dialogue includes such riveting lines as:

> *Whistle wild wind, and whip the wagon on. Slash with your stinging rain your stubborn cart. . . . Blowing through*

---

8 He does worry, however, about places like London, where a brand can buy out a bar for as long as a year and, for a six-figure sum, guarantee a total monopoly.

< 74 >

the flowing stream, the piper conjures in the air forms as fragile as a dream. . . . Moving forward we can still look back and measure our days by the movement of the sun.

The same spirit draws two women, centuries apart. A series of flashbacks reveals that this gin transcends time . . . or that one of these women is possibly schizophrenic. It's a bit frivolous, which is why, distillery ambassador Dennis Tamse informs me, I am one of only a handful of people who have seen it. Considering the current economic climate, the distillery decided to postpone the grand debut for this lavish production—another wise decision. In the meantime, Bob's sons enjoy watching cartoons in the theater.

In a top-floor lounge, connected to the windmill, visiting bartenders can enjoy panoramic views and experiment with cocktails using the vast resources of Diageo: Baileys Irish Cream, Bushmills Irish Whiskey, Captain Morgan Rum, Johnnie Walker Scotch, and Tanqueray Gin, among others. Yes, they can even tinker with the Johnnie Walker Blue Label. But the venue also conducts tastings.

On each placemat sit six sipping glasses, partially filled with vodka, all with lids: Ketel and two competitors on one side, Ketel One Citroen and two other flavored brands on the other. Dennis Tamse and I start with the flagship. Bob tells us to lift the lids and get a whiff of it. Instinctually I swirl the glass around, though I doubt it makes much difference. Following instructions we take a sip, swish it around, and swallow. Bob holds out his palm to represent the tongue and points to where we feel the texture in our mouths. He's right; it's

< 75 >

all-encompassing. The next sample isn't bad: There's a minerality to it, but the mouthfeel isn't as extensive. This is Absolut. The third is unremarkable and turns out to be Grey Goose.

We move to the other side of the mat for the flavored samples. Ketel One Citroen has floral, perfumy notes—and I can't believe I'm thinking about vodka this way either, but it's true. It's pleasant on the palate and tastes nowhere near as strong as it smells. *This would go great on the rocks with club soda,* I think. The second flavored vodka has less presence with a slightly duller hint of citrus. This is Absolut Citron. The third, Grey Goose Le Citron, seemed way too sugary, though I guess it wouldn't matter much in a Grey Goose Cosmopolitan.

I tend not to like Ketel One at room temperature. In a completely blind taste test of four brands back in April 2011, I ranked it dead last. But matched against these rivals, honestly I preferred it. That didn't surprise one craft distiller who immediately guessed the other two brands correctly despite not even being there. He just knew I'd prefer it against those two. "They positioned it well," he said.

How much of that was the power of suggestion? Naturally conversant, Bob conducts the tasting effortlessly. It's easy to go along with him in this carefully crafted process. He also kindly gave me a primer with talking points that would enable me to do tastings of my own. The stiff brochure even serves as the placemat.

The talking points include the four Fs: fragrance, flavor, feel, and finish. Let's take feel by way of example: "The physical impression of a liquid in the mouth," the brochure elucidates. "How does it feel in your mouth? Is it thin,

< 76 >

mouth-coating, smooth?" Finish: "The sensation remaining in the mouth and throat after having swallowed vodka. What are you left with?"

The "Performing Your Tasting" section takes pains in its earnestness. You will find no cheap shots directed, say, at another vodka from Northern Europe: "When performing a Ketel One tasting, we feel it is important that each vodka is treated with respect." But they don't really have to launch any cheap shots. By and large the vodka sells itself. With the possible exception of the ultra-wheat spirits angle, Ketel One tends to avoid the usual marketing ploys, such as how many times it is distilled.

"Those people that say five times, I've tried to find out what they actually say," Bob says. "They see five columns, and they say, 'Oh, five-times distilled.' That's their reasoning. There's now a brand that says hundreds of times distilled—that's even better than five." He elaborates: "Every plate is distillation, so hundreds of times distilled—okay, where is this going? If you're really honest, all vodka needs columns because you need columns to get to neutral grain spirits, and it depends on where you are, if you have five columns or ten, if you can't build them so high, probably more columns you need. But it's one system." Other gimmicky descriptions he has seen include "filtered over diamond dust, a million-years-old glacial water, yeah, there's a lot of things going on."

But what about the jenever that got them started? Surely it, too, would hit big in the United States. Bob tempers his reaction: "When Americans are here, they try it. They say, 'It is amazing!' They love it. Then they go back home. Maybe we

< 77 >

give a bottle. Two years later when you visit them, the bottle is still full because they don't know what it is. They don't know how to drink it." He estimates it will take another twenty years, when his children are in charge.

"We are never in a hurry," says Bob, and he means it. They really aren't. The first national print ads for Ketel One in the United States didn't happen until 2003, after the vodka passed the million-case mark.[9] Then came "Gentlemen, this is vodka," which focused not only on the male demographic but also drinking vodka on the rocks. "If we want to claim basically to be the best vodka available, you should show that this could be drunk neat," Bob insists. "You don't need anything else. Just good ice and nothing else. No vermouth, any fruits, nothing." More recently came a series of commercials directed by Oscar nominee David O. Russell (*The Fighter, Silver Linings Playbook, American Hustle*).

It all comes from the master plan enshrined in Carolus Nolet's three tenets: step by step, no mistakes, keep it simple. His other piece of advice? Don't worry so much about the competition. "If we do what we do right, we'll be okay."

With an extra $900 million, the Nolets are doing more than okay. Ketel One continues to spread across the globe— Australia, Brazil, and Canada are clamoring for the brand. Who knows?—maybe one day Ketel One will even grace bar shelves in Holland.

---

9 It was a simple thank-you note that, according to market tests, not everyone got.

< 78 >

"Vodka is a very small market" in Holland, Bob reveals. It represents about 10 percent of the larger jenever market. "The consumer has to get used to cocktails. When they enter a good cocktail bar and they don't see any beers, don't see any glasses of wine, they see cocktails, they say, 'Okay, I'll try one.' Then they drink cocktails all night." He sees this trend developing in the hotels and bars around Amsterdam, and from these bartender communities in the north, it will spread.

Just like the Borg in *Star Trek*, resistance to Ketel One is futile.

< 79 >

6
SKYY'S THE LIMIT

I lost a tooth! I married a whore!
—Stu Price in *The Hangover*

According to the Mayo Clinic, "a hangover is a group of unpleasant signs and symptoms that can develop after drinking too much alcohol."

"Unpleasant"? Tell that to the guys at a Vegas bachelor party in *The Hangover,* who must piece together the disastrous night before in order to relocate the groom, the mother of a baby in their possession, and the owner of a tiger in their penthouse suite. They're battling headaches, muscle pains, and memory loss caused by alcohol laced with Rohypnol.

"Why don't we remember a goddamn thing from last night?" asks Stu, who married a dancer and extracted his own tooth.

"Obviously because we had a great fucking time," replies Phil, clueless as to why he's wearing a hospital bracelet.

The film became box office gold. It cost $35 million to make and grossed more than $467 million worldwide. But

< 81 >

Maurice Kanbar, creator of SKYY vodka. *BT1 WENN Photos/Newscom*

it's also probably the only time a hangover has been good. For the rest of us, as the Mayo Clinic notes, it means dealing with body aches, dizziness, exhaustion, fatigue, irritability, nausea, sensitivity to light and sound, shakiness, thirst, and even vomiting. "As a general rule," the clinic's website explains, "the more alcohol you drink, the more likely you are to have a hangover the next day. But there's no magic formula to tell you how much you can safely drink and still avoid a hangover."

Maurice Kanbar argues that a magic formula does exist, and it's called quadruple distillation plus triple filtration, a proprietary method of reducing the amount of impurities in vodka to fewer than ten parts per million. Others have replicated the process since, but the Brooklyn-born inventor—known for the D-Fuzz-It sweater comb and the Quad Cinema

< 82 >

multiplex among other innovations—simply wanted a solution to the hangover problem.

Some time in the late 1980s, Kanbar was talking to a physician friend about the vicious headaches he got from even the most minor drinking occasions. "While many suffer a hangover the morning after, I was prone to pounding headaches a few hours after just a drink or two," he reveals in *Secrets from an Inventor's Notebook: How to Turn a Good Idea into a Fortune*. His doctor explained to him the role of congeners. "They give color, flavor, and bouquet. They're present in clear spirits to a lesser degree than in the colored ones, but even small amounts can irritate you."

"Ethyl alcohol is what we want," writes Kanbar, "but, when alcoholic products are not distilled sufficiently, we end up with amyl, butyl, propyl, and isoamyl alcohol, plus acetaldehyde, ethyl formate, and methanol." A distiller informed him that theoretically it was possible to remove more of these congeners than was being done at the time, but everywhere Kanbar went he heard: "We don't need another vodka. There are plenty of vodkas" and "There's no demand for a cleaner spirit. We've been making vodka this way for years."

Despite having no background in the cutthroat spirits industry, Kanbar set out to make his own vodka, a process that lasted almost five years. The labeling alone took nine months. Finding the right bottle, in cobalt blue, took even longer. As for the name, Kanbar briefly considered Prince Nikolai and Czar Alexander, invoking the marketing experts who told Absolut that vodkas with Russian-sounding names would sell better. Mercifully he thought better of these. When he looked out from his window one day and saw a clear blue

< 83 >

sky, it hit him: SKYY. It represented the unquestionable clarity of the vodka, and the second "Y" made the word unique and therefore able to be trademarked (since you can't trademark common words). Plus, as he put it, "It worked for Exxon, didn't it?"

He launched the new vodka in 1992 in San Francisco. Just under a decade earlier, Ketel One came to market at the BIX Restaurant and Supper Club and had steadily grown into a nationally recognized brand, thanks to distributors who begged to carry the Nolets' vodka. Kanbar had the opposite experience. "We simply couldn't get anyone to take us on," he writes in *Secrets from an Inventor's Notebook*. "The San Francisco Bay Area was our initial test market, and, between that smallish market and our lack of a track record, the big distributors we approached turned us away with, 'Why should we have our sales force promote you when we have Absolut?'"

Mirroring the Ketel One strategy, Kanbar focused on the bartenders and getting them to do the selling for him. Like Absolut's Peter Ekelund, who went block by block in Manhattan promoting the Swedish brand, Kanbar rode his scooter around to different drinking establishments and liquor stores offering to do taste tests, pitting more expensive imports against this affordable domestic vodka, "distilled in America from American grain." It worked like a charm.

To prove his commitment to the brand, Kanbar promised purveyors that, if they bought SKYY at the wholesale price, he would buy back at the retail price whatever didn't sell in a week. "I never wound up having to buy a bottle of SKYY at retail," he recalls. SKYY appeared at celebrity and charity

< 84 >

events and made its way onto the *Late Show with David Letterman.* A guest chef used the vodka in a cooking demo, and for laughs Letterman took a few swigs from the cobalt blue bottle—the kind of publicity that money can't buy. The *Star* tabloid reported that "the new Hollywood fad is a brand of vodka, which is supposed to be hangover-free" and that Jack Nicholson, one of its biggest fans, "has it delivered to his house." The story ran in the *Star,* so Kanbar really wasn't sure if Nicholson did order it, but after the story ran he sent a case over to the home of the Oscar-winning actor.

But that line about SKYY being "hangover-free" drew the attention of the Bureau of Alcohol, Tobacco, and Firearms, leading the ATF to demand Kanbar rescind the claim. In all fairness, Kanbar had never gone that far. In a June 1992 write-up, the *San Francisco Examiner* pointed out that the proprietary distillation process "isn't intended for heavy drinkers" and that Kanbar "isn't promising a hangover-free morning if you drink mass quantities." In November 1994 Kanbar told the *Philadelphia Inquirer* that he wasn't "guaranteeing that you won't get a headache" and that "If you drink enough of SKYY or any other vodka, you are going to get a headache and possibly cirrhosis of the liver." In his book, published in 2001, he notes again that "we can't promise 'purity' or guarantee no 'hangovers,'" and you'll find no mention of hangovers in any SKYY ad.

Unlike Absolut's bottle-centric series and Ketel One's opaque thank-you notes, SKYY took the sensual route. One ad features a woman sitting on a bed next to a martini. She is gesturing as if explaining something to her dark-suited husband, whom we see only partially from the side. Another man, smeared lipstick on his face, is hiding underneath the bed.

< 85 >

The SKYY ad was called "Skin Tight."

He, too, is holding a martini glass. A bottle of SKYY sits on the rug. The ad is called "Hidden Agenda." Another, called "The Proposal," shows a woman dressed all in black, including leather pants, on her knees holding a martini glass up to another girl, dressed in red. Another still, for SKYY Melon, called "Wet," features a woman clad in a white bikini at the edge of a pool, helping herself to a SKYY Melon martini and looking . . . well, wet.

By the end of the decade, SKYY had become the third best-selling premium vodka in the United States. In 2001, seven years before Diageo did the same with Ketel One, Maurice Kanbar agreed to sell 50 percent of SKYY to Gruppo Campari for approximately $200 million. Kanbar sold his remaining stake to Campari in 2005. Abiding by a three-year non-compete clause, the octogenarian inventor recently came out with Blue Angel Vodka, which he hopes consumers will use in a martini and refer to as BAM. Needless to say, it hasn't taken off the way "SKYY and soda" did. Meanwhile, SKYY continues to sell roughly 2.7 million cases in America each year, outpacing Ketel One but still trailing Absolut.

So what has life been like at SKYY without Maurice Kanbar?

In the fall of 2012 the Embarcadero neighborhood of San Francisco still hosted SKYY headquarters, across the street from Pier 39 and the aquarium.[10] Inconspicuous from the outside, the company shared the floor with an architecture firm. But opening that plain-white door, I encounter a different

---

10 It has moved since.

< 87 >

world inside. It is very much like the scene in *The Simpsons* when Bart visits *Mad* magazine: A glimpse within reveals Alfred E. Neuman and more mayhem, bells, and whistles than anyone could have imagined.

The lights burn dim, the furnishings look sleek, and a long bar to the right displays all the products of the Campari family: Appleton Estate rum, the Italian apéritifs Cinzano and Campari, Wild Turkey bourbon, and rows of cobalt blue. Straight ahead through a wall of glass lies the conference room, also filled with SKYY bottles. On the back wall is the image of actress Gretchen Mol . . . possibly. When asked to confirm her identity, the receptionist replies, "I don't know who she is."

"That's correct," says Maura McGinn, global head of spirits for Campari, adding, "She's older now. That would have been late 1990s, I'm guessing." Mol starred in *Rounders, The Notorious Betty Page,* and *Boardwalk Empire* and looks, quite simply, luscious. The photo, however, has been enhanced. She looks almost painted as she sits at a table, one hand caressing the top of a martini glass, the other holding up a pin about to burst a bubble. Her mouth hangs seductively half open. Matthew Rolston took the photo, entitled "Bubble Lounge."

Most guys would kill to have Maura McGinn's job. For the last four years the California native has worked for Gruppo Campari. She studied political science and French literature at Berkeley but eventually went into marketing. She lived in Ireland for a time working for Guinness, a part of the Diageo empire. Now this. Aside from overseeing the Scotches, whiskeys, and brands with lurid names like X-Rated Fusion

< 88 >

"Bubble Lounge" starring Gretchen Mol.
Photo by Matthew Rolston

Liqueur—not to mention Cabo Wabo tequila, brainchild of Van Halen frontman Sammy Hagar—McGinn watches over SKYY. While the brand continues to do great volume, you're more likely to find it on a lower shelf or even the speedrail these days than on the top shelf rubbing shoulders with Ketel One or Chopin. McGinn's job is to stanch this slide.[11]

SKYY was meant to be a super-premium vodka here, priced above the value brands but not exorbitantly so. But then others came along. McGinn likens this to a pileup. "You either have to keep up with that challenge, keep increasing your prices, or . . . naturally get pushed down in perception." She compares pricing to gravity: "It's difficult to keep on increasing your price if people kind of lock into a certain price point." Suddenly, in her words, your Banana Republic has become a Gap, and before long it's turned into an Old Navy. Looking back, she says, "We should've responded somewhat, but you had brands deliberately coming out and charging fifty dollars a bottle. It changed the frame of reference for vodka. As a result, the category has really evolved."

So has the bar scene. McGinn describes the current setup in trendy locales as consisting of only two tiers: high-end brands on the shelf and no-names in the well. There isn't a middle, and SKYY may end up on the rail. The notion doesn't sit well with her. The upside is the off-premise: liquor stores that have five price categories for vodka. There SKYY

---

11 SKYY is booming in Brazil and South Africa, though, where the vodka has a reputation as a super-premium bottle-service brand.

< 90 >

dominates. The price is reasonable, and the consumer isn't out to impress; she just wants to bring a bottle home for a drink with friends over for dinner. Studies show that the older we get the more we entertain at home and the less we go out to those trendy watering holes.

The problem is that the decision about what to purchase at the store often takes place at the bar first. My decision to drink SKYY at the bar is precisely because of its reasonable price, a happy medium between the plastic-jug value brands and the pretentiously overpriced varieties endorsed by celebrities. My admission comes as cold comfort to her: "We don't want to be a rational choice, an in-between," she tells me. "We almost don't feel the need to bring up the money equation because it will naturally come up anyway. But we don't want to become this rational middle ground choice because that goes the opposite way of why people choose vodka. Price is part of it, but it's not the key driver because it's such a lifestyle choice."

Of course she's right.[12] McGinn admits that SKYY "is good value, but we don't want to be Toyota. No bad remark on Toyota, but we want to focus more on what we offer." What SKYY seems to offer is style rather than status. "Those might sound one and the same, but they are distinct segment groups, and you play in one or the other," she explains. "If you want to play in real status, you're a high price point below volume. If you're

---

12 As we'll see in an upcoming chapter, rational decision making has nothing to do with what vodka to drink in Las Vegas.

< 91 >

more style, you're a lower price point and more accessible. There's not one right way, but there's money to be made in their interaction."

Nor does the equation take origin into consideration, either. No one is ordering SKYY because of its San Francisco roots or because of where it is distilled, which turns out to be at the Wild Turkey distillery in Lawrenceburg, Kentucky. It all seems a bit vague, but McGinn happily elaborates: "With a lot of brands, you can either lock into, okay, it's a male target, it's a female target. Whereas, with SKYY and why it's so big, is that it's actually this perfect intersection of men and women and how men and women actually interact. A whiskey moment is usually among a tight group of males, but vodka has always been capturing that kind of dressing up, the male putting on a little bit more effort in that."

McGinn calls this "the vodka moment."

"We actually did something interesting this year in that we focused on product quality," she says. McGinn knows that SKYY drinkers don't want to hear "a brand ambassador talk yarns about vodka," but they do "want to know it's a very good-quality product. . . . At the end of the day we have other reasons we choose vodka to deliver on that, but ultimately you're selling me the whole deal. You're selling me the experience of vodka."

Like Bob Nolet, McGinn also ridicules competitors who tout the number of times their spirit is distilled. "Is that like an SPF factor where over 30 it just becomes diminishing returns? Is it really that beneficial?" she asks rhetorically. Instead, SKYY launched a campaign called Passion for Perfection, which "talked a little bit about our quality but in a

SKYY way. . . . Ultimately what they're going to SKYY for is that kind of lifestyle look. But they wanted some reassurance. The product is now twenty years old, so it was kind of a way to introduce that story. . . . It was a little bit of a response to what's been going on in the category, to stand up for ourselves a little bit and—we couldn't talk to people about congeners, the old story—to remind people why it is still a great product."

It *is* still a great product, especially for the price. But selling vodka successfully requires a lot more than that. Will Passion for Perfection work? Can SKYY capture "the vodka moment" and "the experience of vodka"? Maybe—but it's easy to get caught up in the ad-speak. It might help if occasionally everyone kept in mind that pearl of wisdom from SKYY's founder, Maurice Kanbar: "Thou shalt not bullshit thyself."

< 93 >

7

THE GREATEST VODKA
STORY EVER TOLD

The nice thing about vodka is you make it today, you sell it tomorrow.

—SIDNEY FRANK, CREATOR OF GREY GOOSE,

TO *INC.* MAGAZINE IN 2005

By 1996 the vodka aisle was getting full. Aside from Smirnoff, the volume giant, the other power players included Absolut, Stolichnaya, SKYY, and Finlandia. That year, the latest most expensive brand hit the market, a Polish vodka called Belvedere, which positioned itself *above* the premium category. It identified itself as super-premium: made with Dankowskie gold rye and distilled four times using filtered artesian well water. To this day it calls itself "the world's first luxury vodka."

None of this deterred Sidney Frank, though, who had been trying to come up with his own vodka at the time. Then, one early morning in the summer of 1996, it hit him. The liquor importer from New Rochelle woke with a start and called his associate to tell him the name of their new vodka: Grey Goose.

< 95 >

It would be unlike anything the spirits industry had ever encountered. Frank was seventy-six years old at the time.

Although Frank's company was based in Westchester County, New York, the vodka would come from Cognac, France, because, as he told Stephanie Clifford of *Inc.,* "France has the best of everything." We associate it with good food, fine wine, cultural treasures, and, of course, attractive women with seductive accents. They would distill from the same wheat used in those flaky, delicate French pastries. The water would filter through Champagne limestone, emphasis on the *Champagne.*

The packaging would come in a tall, frosted glass bottle with a long neck, hence the name. With the exception of those ridiculous bottles of Galliano liqueur (vital for those Harvey Wallbangers), it would

Sidney Frank relaxes at his San Diego home in 2004. © *Robyn Twomey/Corbis*

The original Grey Goose.
Courtesy of Grey Goose

< 97 >

stand out as the tallest item on the bar shelf, making it particularly easy for bartenders to grab—remember the common complaint about Absolut's short neck?—and it would cost almost double what Absolut did. Grey Goose first sold for thirty dollars a bottle. Frank guessed that consumers would think that, if it was expensive, it must be good. He was right.[13]

According to the critics, Grey Goose was, in fact, better: In 1998 the Beverage Testing Institute conferred on Grey Goose the title of Best Tasting Vodka in the World. Frank quickly capitalized on the distinction, telling *Inc.*

> *We took $3 million, which was going to be our total profit for a year, and we put it into advertising. We made big, beautiful ads that listed Grey Goose as the best-tasting vodka in the world, and we indoctrinated the distributors and 20,000 bartenders, and when somebody would come in and say, "What's your best-tasting vodka?" they said Grey Goose.*

As we saw a century earlier, Pyotr Smirnov instructed his workers to go into bars throughout Russia, demanding Smirnov's vodka by name in an early version of a word-of-mouth campaign. Once he garnered the endorsement of Czar Alexander III in 1886, he quickly took advantage. "The very next day," writes Linda Himelstein in *The King of Vodka*,

---

13 This time-tested market logic also helped universities struggling with declining applications. In 2000 Ursinus College in Pennsylvania raised its tuition by more than 17 percent and watched as its entering class grew by 35 percent over four years. As the *New York Times* pointed out, "Applicants had apparently assumed that if the college cost more, it must be better."

< 98 >

"Smirnov ordered that all his labels be changed to carry the new distinction."

Later the Nolets instituted educational workshops for distributors and bartenders for Ketel One. Sidney Frank wasn't breaking new ground; he was following time-honored tradition.

The BTI endorsement was a well-crafted bit of publicity. The blind taste test involved forty vodkas with points awarded for characteristics such as smoothness and taste, true, but Frank had hired the institute to conduct the test. Grey Goose scored a 96 on a 100-point scale while Absolut received an 80. "There were nearly twenty vodkas in between, some that I honestly had never even heard of and wondered if they actually existed," writes Richard Lewis in *Absolut Sequel.* "Grey Goose built its brand on the shoulders of this single test result. They created one annoying ad and ran it hundreds of times—and it worked. Many ad professionals describe the taste test ad as cheesy, gauche, or distasteful." Still, he gives them credit. "They stayed on message. Grey Goose became what it set out to be: the world's best-tasting vodka."

Those millions spent on marketing Grey Goose paid off. It appeared at awards shows like the Emmys as well as at charitable events.[14] Word got around until finally the brand made its way onto *Sex and the City,* where Carrie, Samantha,

---

14 The Grey Goose Emmy cocktail consists of 1½ parts Grey Goose Le Citron, ½ part cucumber juice, ½ part fresh lime juice, 1 part St. Germain. Shake with ice, strain into martini glass, and serve with rosemary sprig and edible silver flakes. Don't ask me where to buy those flakes.

< 99 >

Charlotte, and Miranda specifically drank Grey Goose Cosmos. As Seth Stevenson put it in *New York* magazine: "In the battle for vodka supremacy, this was the atom bomb. The war was over. Grey Goose had won."

But, as we saw at the beginning of our journey, not all the publicity surrounding Grey Goose has been good. In 2006 Maurice Clarett, the former Ohio State tailback, led police on a chase through Columbus, ending in a restaurant parking lot. He had in his car three handguns, an AK-47 assault rifle, a samurai sword, a box of condoms, and an empty bottle of Grey Goose. In 2012, in that brawl inside the Double Seven nightclub, Adam Hock knocked out Stavros Niarchos and clocked Pierre Casiraghi, before a member of the prince's entourage hit Hock over the head with a bottle of Grey Goose.

But no matter. Each year, Grey Goose sells approximately 3.8 million cases around the world. It's the second most-imported vodka in the United States behind Absolut, and, as we soon will see, it's the most popular vodka in Las Vegas. To put it in SKYY terms, it has managed to have both style *and* status. It has become a top-shelf brand that does heavy volume. It's practically everywhere.

Case in point: A prominent advertising executive spoke of a recent visit to the Virgin Atlantic Clubhouse at Heathrow Airport. "We go into the clubhouse in London yesterday, and it's unbelievable," he says. "The food is unbelievable. It's set up like an adult clubhouse. You can go into one room, and there're pool tables. You go into another room, there's nothing but technology. It is phenomenal. It really is. Then the *pièce de résistance* . . . is when you go up this flight of steps, and . . . in their clubhouses they have a bar, and that bar is

< 100 >

Grey Goose. It's a *Grey Goose* bar . . . so I guess you can have it with ice or without ice," he says with a hearty laugh. Virgin Atlantic's website describes the Grey Goose Loft as "the ultimate preflight indulgence."

This vodka, proudly "distilled and bottled in France" in a region that had no tradition of distilling vodka, has become one of the great success stories of the industry. For Sidney Frank, the American Dream had come true.

Born in 1919, Frank grew up poor on a farm in Montville, Connecticut, about eighty miles east of Bethel, where Rudolph Kunett opened the first vodka distillery in America. Frank's mother made the family's bedsheets by sewing together flour sacks. Embracing the farm philosophy of "Make it or make do," he cultivated an entrepreneurial spirit. At nearby Cochegan Rock, Frank brought a ladder to assist tourists who wanted a better view from the top. He charged a dime per person. He was twelve years old at the time.

Frank was smart enough to attend Brown University, next door in Rhode Island, but he could afford only a year's tuition. Still, he had the good fortune of rooming with Edward Sarnoff, whose father, David Sarnoff, was president of RCA. On a visit to the Sarnoff home, Frank slept on cotton sheets for the first time. In that instant, as he later said to *Forbes,* "I knew I had to marry a rich girl"—which he did. "After proposing six times," writes *Forbes*'s Matthew Miller, "Frank finally convinced Louise Rosenstiel to marry him in the late 1940s." Louise's father, Lewis Rosenstiel, ran Schenley Distillers Corporation, then the country's largest liquor distributor. Schenley predominantly distributed brown spirits, such as Old Quaker and Black Velvet whiskeys.

< 101 >

After a stint at Connecticut-based aviation manufacturer Pratt & Whitney during World War II, where he worked on jet fuel, Frank joined his father-in-law's business and was quickly dispatched to London to rescue a flagging Scotch operation. As he recalled to *Forbes,* "The guys who sold us the operation were only making a million gallons per week. We made 3.6 million gallons. There was a difference of $10 million per week staring them right in the face. I just did the obvious."

His relationship with his father-in-law eventually soured, and by the time Louise died in 1973 Frank had struck out on his own. He had a rocky start, though. It took him seven years to turn a profit, but then Frank saw an opportunity: Trusting his instincts, he acquired a digestif popular in the German immigrant community called Jägermeister. At the time, only about six hundred cases were selling each year.

In the 1980s, however, it became enormously popular in college bars, mostly in the South. Students nicknamed it Liquid Valium. Some considered it an aphrodisiac. It didn't hurt that Frank dispatched attractive Jägerettes to hawk the liqueur: "I thought a pretty girl can always help you selling," he told *Inc.,* "and I noticed that one girl in California would go to 80 tables in a room and say, 'Open your mouth.' She asked, 'Would you like a Jägermeister?' and 80 percent of 'em said yes."[15]

---

15 Initially, says Frank, the women suspected him of recruiting for a "house of ill repute." Though obviously not the case, the company did settle a lawsuit in 1997—in which former Jägerettes claimed to have been sexually harassed—to the tune of $2.6 million.

< 102 >

Jägermeister remains one of Sidney Frank Importing's marquee products. It has become the best-selling imported liqueur in America, from six hundred cases each year to more than one million—an astounding feat for something that tastes so godawful. As Ted Wright of the beverage marketing firm Liquid Intelligence told *New York* magazine, Jägermeister "is a liqueur with an unpronounceable name. It's drunk by older, blue-collar Germans as an after-dinner digestive aid. It's a drink that on a good day is an acquired taste. If Sidney Frank can make that drink synonymous with 'party'—which he has—he can pretty much do anything."

So it should have come as no surprise that Frank would create a vodka distilled in France, charge twice the going rate, and boost sales well above three million cases in the span of less than a decade. For a time, it was the fastest-growing spirit in history. Only P. Diddy's Ciroc has grown faster.

Frank always wanted to be a billionaire, and in 2004 he finally became one when he sold Grey Goose to Bacardi for $2.3 billion. By then, at age eighty-five, he was already living a comfortable life. In no physical condition to play golf, Frank still led a team of aspiring pros around a golf course in New York State, paying them to play while dispensing advice. As *Forbes* explained, "In addition to their $50,000 salaries, Frank would pay his pros cash after every hole: $1,000 for a double eagle, $500 for eagle, $100 for birdie—plus $500 to the round's winner."

After selling Grey Goose, Frank worried that his employees would look elsewhere for work. As a preventive measure the company gave out bonuses. Those who had been with

< 103 >

Sidney Frank Importing for ten years received a whopping two-year bonus. No one left.

But he did buy two Maybachs, luxury cars made by Daimler (since discontinued). "Not the little ones," he told *Inc.* "In one of the Maybachs, if you sit in the back seat and press a button, it extends like a bed."[16] Sadly, Frank enjoyed his billionaire status for less than two years. He died on January 10, 2006.

What happened after the success of Grey Goose, we can describe only as a vodka boom. Within a matter of years, the number of brands on the market went from a few hundred to over a thousand. But rather than crowding one another out, the entire market has grown both in volume and profit. Revenue from higher-priced brands has risen dramatically. According to data from the Distilled Spirits Council of the United States, in 2003 Americans spent $320 million on super-premium vodkas. In 2012 we spent $1.2 billion on the category. In other words, spending $30 on a bottle of neutral grain spirits no longer seems absurd.

Why did so many rush into the business? Part of the reason, of course, was the tantalizing price tag for Grey Goose. Selling anything for $2.3 billion is an entrepreneur's dream come true—though getting to that point requires much more than many aspiring distillers realize.

John Frank, Sidney's nephew and vice chairman of Sidney Frank Importing, reflects on the so-called Grey Goose

---

16 At the time, a Maybach 62 S—one of the "not the little ones"—cost approximately $430,000.

< 104 >

Model. "Sidney was always a big thinker and one to ask, 'Why not?' especially if it involved a healthy margin," Frank tells me. Regarding Grey Goose Vodka, "it was a case of almost perfect aspirational marketing. We wanted to provide consumers with affordable luxury and knew that the product had to be of the highest quality with exquisite packaging, but also that the timing had to be right." He notes that they "employed tough price margin discipline, never giving in to sales volume price pressure, and constantly worked on quality distribution while promoting the brand at upscale, glamorous, and charitable events."

In short, a variety of factors—some of which depend simply on sheer luck—have to go right in order to pull off such massive success. "Grey Goose was the right product for the right time," says Frank, "but it was also the culmination of twenty-five years of building brands and a strong sales-distribution organization." It may turn out that no one can replicate the Grey Goose story, but the tale offers enough inspiration to convince risk-takers to take that plunge—even if the current vodka scene is, as described by one industry insider, "Sutter's Mill, 1850."

"Work hard. Extra hard," Frank told Brown University's alumni magazine in 2004. "If you meet any important people, keep in touch with them. Work for a big company before starting your own, just so you can get experience."[17]

Sidney Frank had vision and formidable business acumen, remarkable traits for someone who not only lacked a business

---

[17] "And marry a rich girl," he added. "It's easier to marry a million than to make a million."

< 105 >

degree but who never even made it past his freshman year in college. But he didn't need a diploma from an Ivy League institution in order to live the American Dream. Nor did he harbor any animosity toward his alma mater for not providing him with financial aid. Before he died, Frank gifted $100 million to Brown University.

Sidney Frank represents the greatest success story in the world of vodka. But he wasn't alone. As Grey Goose was taking flight, another vodka story was taking shape, of all places, down in the foothills of Texas.

< 106 >

8

THE LEGEND OF TITO BEVERIDGE

I always looked at it like a filet mignon at a pot-roast price.
—TITO BEVERIDGE ON TITO'S HANDMADE VODKA

At Austin-Bergstrom International Airport, it doesn't take long to realize you have entered the land of Tito's Handmade Vodka. It took me only a matter of minutes. Our plane had just reached the gate, and as we were waiting to disembark I told my seatmate that I was going to interview the man behind this Texas vodka. A fellow passenger waiting in the aisle overheard me and said, "It's the best! They distill it six times"—true—"from potatoes"—false. "It's really smooth," which I was about to find out.

On the way to the hotel, my taxi turns onto Highway 71. Amid the brown hills and scrub brush, a billboard suddenly appears: WELCOME TO AUSTIN, HOME OF TITO'S HANDMADE VODKA.

His full name is Bert Butler Beveridge II—Little Bert, Bertito, Tito—and that's really his last name, too. But the beverage business wasn't Beveridge's first calling in life. He had

< 107 >

several callings after he graduated from the University of Texas in 1984. Although he had majored in pre-med studies, as he explained in the *New York Times,* "I didn't like being around sick people." Data processing bored him, so he did the opposite one summer and worked on an oil rig. Eventually he joined Western Geophysical and headed to South America looking for natural gas, a process involving dynamite and geophone arrays that he likens to taking an ultrasound of the Earth. He briefly worked in the drilling business back in the United States, moved on to environmental cleanup, and ended up in real estate.

At which point Tito happened to catch a show on PBS about career paths. The host said the way to find your ideal job was to make two columns, one listing what you like doing and the other listing what you did well. Tito was good at selling mortgages, but it wasn't exactly fun. On the other hand, he had always enjoyed making alcohol, whether brewing beer in college or, more recently, creating habanero-infused vodkas for his friends. That's how Tito chose to distill vodka for a living.

But Tito lacked a background in the distilling business. He didn't know anything about federal regulations and distribution. Established brands competed fiercely for market share. No legal distillery existed in the state. Somehow this thirty-two-year-old was supposed to acquire the first permit, operate several stills, handle the bottling, and convince people to drink vodka from Texas? Good luck.

But luck he had, not to mention persistence. From a thousand cases in 1997 to close to a million today, with distribution agreements in all fifty states, Tito Beveridge is living the

American Dream, yet another iconic figure to inspire count-less others to join the vodka boom. But the more you learn about Tito, the more you realize that this business isn't for the faint of heart. It takes a certain type of person: one who has experienced failure, will risk everything, and isn't afraid to deal with the Alcohol and Tobacco Tax and Trade Bureau.

The distillery lies about fourteen miles southeast of downtown and just south of the airport. It's in the middle of nowhere. Across the way you'll find a Mexican-style rodeo. No large sign welcomes visitors to the home of Tito's Hand-made Vodka. Aside from the address—which I was sworn not to reveal—the first thing you'll see is the barbed-wire fence enclosing the distillery and the guard house. An armed secu-rity officer asks for my name and escorts me past the elec-tronic gate to the office. Suddenly dogs are barking—*big* dogs. One is a black lab, the other a brown pit mix, the third a boxer. If you didn't already know this was a vodka distillery, you might think it a nuclear missile site.[18]

The office is a shack of sorts, the interior a mess of papers, bottles, and random trophies. On the wall hang a few pictures and various newspaper clippings. On the desk stands a min-iature pot still. Safe to say, this isn't the Nolet Distillery. When Tito walks in, much to the delight of the dogs, he looks exactly as he appears in the ads: blue button-down shirt, jeans, and cowboy boots. His hair is more salt than pepper these days.

---

[18] The security perimeter went up after the completion of a nearby toll road. The road unintentionally provided access for meth heads and other thieves to come and break in to steal copper and other valuable metals.

< 109 >

Tanned, he looks in good shape for a fifty-one-year-old who's devoted his life to making booze.

How many cases did he ship last year and what was he expecting this year?

"Uh, there's no tellin'." I prod him further. "Lots and lots," he'll only say vaguely. "There's enough to finally pay off my credit cards," which is a considerable accomplishment. At one point Tito had nineteen credit cards and $70,000 in debt. No one wanted to invest.

For a while it was literally a one-man operation—distilling, bottling, labeling (using Elmer's Glue), and packaging to the point of getting carpal tunnel syndrome. "I had a cot out here, and I'd built a shower, and I had some hot plates and a micro-wave and a refrigerator." Many a night he slept next to his still with his dog as his only companion.

So why do it?

"I'd been making flavored vodkas for my friends for Christmas presents," Tito recalls, "and so, when I got into it, I was just kind of like, Wouldn't it be great if I didn't have to work for The Man, and work for myself, doing something that I enjoy doing?" His aim started small: "When I first decided to latch on to this idea, I was like, 'If I could do sixty cases a month and make $20 a case, I could make $1,200 a month and have this great lifestyle, where I could hang out with my dog all day and go to bars and meet girls at night.' I thought, *Man, what a great plan.*"

Tito and best friend Roscoe. *Photo by Knox Photographics*

< 110 >

Carolus Nolet's grand master plan it wasn't.

It soon dawned on Tito that producing vodka wasn't, as he put it, like making hot sauce and selling it at the farmers' market. "As I got into it, I realized it takes a lot more than sixty cases a month. Then, oh my God, it takes a lot more money than I thought that it would. . . . If I had known, I probably wouldn't have done it. But I didn't know. So I just jumped into it."

What Tito did know was the success of the craft brewing industry. "I saw the whole deal that happened in the beer business, where it used to be Schlitz, Miller, and Budweiser, the big boys. Then Coors came out—everybody thought that was a big deal. Then, all of a sudden, it was like, Wow, now there's Indian Pale Ales and these bocks and pilsners, and just this whole explosion. My thought was, *What would happen if you did that in the liquor business?*"

What happened was the rise of the microdistillery. Tito thinks he even may have come up with the word himself. A few mentions of microdistilling predate Tito's Handmade Vodka, the first among them as early as 1988 in a UPI article by Steven Bredice about Vermont Distillers, makers of gin and vodka. Nevertheless, Tito ought to receive credit for paving the way for the little guys—many of whom no longer think of him as little.

Nor is he. Sales have always been steady, even if people complained that his bottles needed to be frosted like Grey

Tito's Handmade vodka. *Photo by Cory Ryan*

< 112 >

Goose's. He also had a few lucky boosts along the way. The first came in the late 1990s when Tony Abou-Ganim, then in charge of developing the cocktail program for the Bellagio in Las Vegas, informed Tito that his vodka was the best that the famed mixologist had ever tasted. Eventually Tito made it over to Sin City and conducted vodka taste test seminars—with his vodka a clear favorite. Then came another blind taste test in 2001 at the San Francisco World Spirits Competition. Tito's won Double Gold, meaning it was the unanimous favorite over every other brand.

But with success in the spirits business comes the ever watchful eye of the Alcohol and Tobacco Tax and Trade Bureau. Tito has survived multiple audits, including one claiming that he committed twenty-six violations and owed the government $3.5 million. "I thought I was going to lose the distillery," he recalls. "I didn't sleep for a year and a half. It was just horrible. Then in the end, I went through my federal code and showed them that I was doing it right." Ultimately, he says, "they told me they might have gotten twenty pounds of flesh off of me but I got a good, solid ten off of them."

He doesn't go into details.

Tito also doesn't get into the details of the sensitive subject of importing neutral grain spirits (NGS). Not every brand does its own in-house fermentation. Distilleries commonly bring in preformulated alcohol, which then they run through additional column or pot stills with additives applied. Even Lars Ohlsson Smith, the man on the Absolut medallion, purchased spirits from Russia, which he filtered back in Sweden. In the United States a handful of ethanol plants in the Midwest and Idaho provide much of the neutral grain spirits used

< 114 >

by vodka makers. Tito supposedly gets his from the Grain Processing Corporation in Muscatine, Iowa, but when asked to confirm this point by e-mail he doesn't reply.

Some critics take umbrage at Tito's claim that he is a micro- or craft distiller when smaller brands pride themselves on making vodka entirely on premise, including fermentation. "I find it egregious that he calls it handmade," says Dave Kyrejko of Industry City Distillery, about whom more later. "If somebody said it was a fully automatic machine-made process, I'd be much more impressed than a handmade, small-batch, artisanal, craft-made process. It's all bullshit, and it's . . . annoying. You don't know who to believe anymore because you can say whatever you want."

"It's cheaper for them," explains Nicholas Spink of Spike Vodka in San Antonio. "If somebody says it's five, six times [distilled], it's because the NGS company is doing it that way. It's the chic word." But again, that doesn't mean NGS importers aren't doing any distilling at all. The government requires you to run it through your still just once in order to put "distilled by" on the label. In the precise words of the Alcohol and Tobacco Tax and Trade Bureau: "A bottler who actually redistills neutral spirits in the production of vodka or who is the proprietor of the production facilities where the eligible neutral spirits were distilled may use on labels the term 'distilled by.'"

According to Spink, "If you look at the cheap brands, and there's a couple out there, they're basically fourteen dollars. It'll say 'bottled by.' All they did is take an NGS and put more water in it to bring it down to 40 percent alcohol, and they don't even filter it. They just put it right into the bottle."

Spink acknowledges that Tito's doesn't do this. "They are a neighbor—we're in San Antonio, and they're in Austin—and they're one of the biggest in Texas. They are what I call an NGS company. There's only two—we have eleven labels in Texas—us and one other vodka are the only ones created on-site. That's it." A European distiller at a significantly larger company describes the rise of Tito's as "amazing," adding that "he started in a garage, it's a true story." But "Of course now with the growth, he's bringing in the neutral grain spirits from outside Texas, so is he then a Texas vodka?"

It's an interesting question and one Tito chooses not to answer. But during my visit he touched on the expansion in the most delicate manner. "At one point there's a big switch for us because we kept growing," he explains. "How do you ever make a bunch of this stuff?—because it's kind of like going to make cookies for the Cub Scout troop. Then all of a sudden Southwest Airlines wants to buy cookies from you. How do you make that transition? It's not easy."

Sam Adams made that transition, though few still consider it a microbrew. The same goes for Tito's, especially as it approaches the million-case mark. Should it matter? When Tito takes me for a tour, he hands me a sample of warm vodka in a test tube with a reading of 40.4 percent alcohol. It's delicious. He hands me a second tube, advising me to take just a tiny sip. It immediately evaporates on the tongue amid a sensation of unbearable heat. This one is 96 percent alcohol. "But you can still taste some of the characteristics, right?" he asks. Yes—in between the flames of hell.

The label undoubtedly will continue to read "Tito's Handmade Vodka" with the description, "Crafted in an Old

< 116 >

Fashioned Pot Still by America's Original Microdistillery" . . . even if it isn't so micro these days. But other aspects of his product Tito doesn't care so much about, such as raising prices. "Half a gallon of Tito's was priced $29.99, and that was in 1999 or 2000," he recalls. "Now you can go to a liquor store, thirteen years later, and it's right around $29.99 and, you know, $32.99. Thirteen years later, and everything's gone up. . . . I've managed to keep the price down just because I've always looked at it like: I started off making it for my friends, and I wanted to be where they could afford it. I always looked at it like a filet mignon at a pot-roast price."

Tito also knows that no one is going to order his vodka for bottle service; it's not Grey Goose. He probably doesn't mind being, in the words of SKYY's Maura McGinn, the Toyota of vodkas. "I don't care if somebody's a blue-collar mechanic, AC repairman, or somebody working for the government or something like that. I'm happy for them. There are some brands that are just like, Those aren't our people. We don't want them. I'm more like, I love those people. The people at the country club, the people who play golf, I love those people, too. People who ride horses and stockbrokers and Wall Street guys and girls, hedge fund people—love those people, too. We love everybody."

What matters most? Tito wants a vodka "that I can drink warm and still have a smile on my face, no burn. You go and put some ice on it, it opens up, like vanilla, caramel notes. Shake it, make a martini, you're just like, Man, this is good vodka, this guy knows what he's doing. You can really enjoy it. That's one part of it."

< 117 >

Second, "Nobody ever talks about the feeling you get from it because different things make you feel differently. I like a feeling that's just nice and smooth and relaxing and easy. I don't ever want to feel like I gotta put my hand up against the wall or I gotta keep my foot down to keep the bed from spinning, none of that. . . . I don't like stupid stuff coming out of my mouth or my wife getting mad at me. I just like nice, easy."

Third, "I like to wake up the next morning and not have a hangover. I just want to get up, cook the kids pancakes, and I can get my work done." It sounds like the "vodka experience" first mentioned at SKYY.

Considering the number of jobs he's held, would he ever leave the distilling world and do something else? Probably not. "I can see being a really old guy and still doing this." By "this" he may not strictly mean vodka. At one point I ask if he ever had an interest in whiskey.

His eyes light up. "I actually enjoy making whiskey, and I like the whole aging process," he says. "You know what, I've been making myself *not* do it for six years now. I mean, I was so close to doing it back then. I bought every whiskey on the market, blind-tasted everything, knew what my favorites were, came up with a whiskey that was better than that, and then I was ready to do it."

But he didn't.

"I think about it all the time," says the fifth-generation Texan, and he says his distributors would love nothing more. But "more than anything I think it would just take my sales-men's focus off what they're doing. The problem we have now, we're just constantly . . . working every batch, and it's enough.

< 118 >

It keeps us really busy all the time." Plus, his wife opposes it.

Still, he hems and haws. "I don't know, I keep threatening to. But then I don't want to. It's kind of like . . . We'll just make it for us to drink. I've got some friends that are making some whiskey. I'm just going to make some to take to them, let them try it." But then he asks himself, "Why do I want to take my eye off this [vodka] to go do something else I don't enjoy as much as this?"

But Tito clearly is itching for it. He admits to ordering a few barrels recently—but he won't be filling them with vodka. He owns the land on both sides of the distillery just in case he wants to construct an aging warehouse. Not that he's interested.

While waiting for a cab to take me back downtown, Tito sits with me on the porch, surrounded by his dogs. He jokes about how the Russians shot their vodka, beat their chests, and yelled out toasts laced with profanity all because the product was so terrible. We look out at the charro rodeo far in the distance. A cowboy gallops around, carrying an American flag. A beer stand is open. Tito laughs that it's probably illegal.

We talk again about the early days, when Tito worked alone on this desolate plain. It reached the point that his friends finally staged a career intervention. They told him that he'd given it his best shot, but sleeping on a cot next to a still and a dog just wasn't healthy. They urged him to go back into real estate. Tito told them that he knew what he was doing— he just needed help. Today he employs seventy workers, and he doesn't miss selling mortgages.

9
HOLLYWOOD

Who do I have to sleep with around here to get a Stoli martini with a twist of lemon?
—CATE BLANCHETT IN WOODY ALLEN'S *BLUE JASMINE*

In 2010 Stolichnaya ran a campaign called "Would you have a drink with you?" One of the ads featured actress Julia Stiles sitting next to actress Julia Stiles, debating the merits of starring in art-house films versus soulless blockbusters. In another, Hugh Hefner meets his sensitive side who says, "Deep down, I'm just a guy like everyone else, looking for love." The other Hef lustily eyes a model on a couch and says, "Love. Really?" Twitter founder Biz Stone pokes fun at himself over mindless tweets about the president's Caesar salad. Of course, everyone's drinking Stoli. The ads feature witty banter and famous people, which may be what it takes to convince someone to order a Stoli and soda at the bar.

On the marketplace battlefield, the celebrity endorsement has become another way to defeat the competition. Thanks

< 121 >

Courtesy of Crystal Head Vodka

to our increasing pop culture obsession, such endorsements probably resonate more than simply a brand's good taste or affordability. Some strongly disagree with this approach, though, like Tito Beveridge. The distillery itself handles all publicity in-house, and he claims zero interest in running glitzy promotions.

On the other hand, SKYY Vodka photographed its bottle next to a slew of famous actors. Belvedere has the backing of comedienne Chelsea Handler, whose own breakout best-selling book was *Are You There, Vodka? It's Me, Chelsea.* Belvedere's value brand, Sobieski, has Bruce Willis. Marking a new direction for Absolut, the latest iteration—Absolut Elyx— isn't just about the bottle, it's also about Chloë Sevigny. Even a small outfit like Americana Vodka, based in Scobeyville, New Jersey, has the support of NFL legend Dan Marino, and Bad Boy Vodka appropriately enough features Dennis Rodman.[19]

---

19 As *USA Today* sports columnist Chris Chase put it, "A perfect representation of Rodman would be a vodka that tastes like hair dye, smells like patchouli and Drakkar Noir, changes color every time it's poured, and can be used to disinfect new piercing areas."

< 122 >

None of this is new. Pyotr Smirnov earned the ultimate endorsement in 1886 from Czar Alexander III, and in the 1950s the Smirnoff company landed a score of talent, including Woody Allen, the Gabor sisters, and Gypsy Rose Lee. But sometimes celebrity endorsements go awry. Rapper-producer Pharrell Williams sued Diageo after they terminated his deal with Qream liqueur, geared toward women. Devotion Vodka's relationship with Mike "The Situation" Sorrentino of *Jersey Shore* fame ended in a legal battle with both sides accusing the other of breach of contract.[20]

In some instances the endorsement can take the form of art. Absolut famously paid Andy Warhol, Keith Haring, Jean-Michel Basquiat, and others to create their interpretations of the brand. Wyborowa commissioned architect Frank Gehry to design the bottle for its single-estate variety. True to Gehry form, it looks like one of those knowledge cylinders used in Superman's Fortress of Solitude. But lately the arrangement has gone beyond a simple blurb in exchange for a flat fee. Now companies offer stock options and even partnership. Bruce Willis is a part-owner of Sobieski.

Perhaps most famously, rapper-entrepreneur P. Diddy received a piece of Ciroc, part of the Diageo empire, back in 2007 when the French grape–distilled vodka was still selling a mere forty thousand cases a year. It has since sold a

---

20 Sorrentino also went to war against Abercrombie & Fitch over its use of the terms "The Fitchuation" and "GTL Fitch." Sorrentino lost the suit, and Abercrombie tried to pay the reality star $10,000 *not* to wear their clothing.

< 123 >

total of over two million cases. In his first three years with Ciroc, P. Diddy helped boost sales by 552 percent, surpassing Belvedere.[21]

Aside from pushing the brand at clubs, Diddy declared Ciroc the official vodka of New Year's Eve. "When the ball drops, if you're not drinking Ciroc Vodka, you're not drinking New Year's Eve the right way," he told the press. He promoted it in a Rat Pack–themed commercial called "Luck Be a Lady," starring Eva Pigford, Michael K. Williams, Aaron Paul, and everyone's favorite mob actor, Frank Vincent (*Casino, Goodfellas, The Sopranos*). As the rapper explained to *Advertising Age,* "It's not a glorified endorsement deal; it's a hands-on, day-to-day investment," one that, according to estimates, has earned him $100 million.

So it came as no surprise in 2008 that legendary actor and funnyman Dan Aykroyd launched his own vodka. Why not? But the video that introduced the new brand couldn't have been more, shall we say, unconventional:

I'm Dan Aykroyd. Since childhood I have been fascinated by the invisible world, a world which can help us get through life if we know how to draw upon its power, a world serving positive projections, wherein you use your own personal, mental, and spiritual abilities to believe and subsequently make true the things that you want to happen for yourself.

---

21 The hip-hop artist may have taken inspiration from 50 Cent, who raked in a staggering $200 million, before taxes, when Glaceau bought his shares of Vitamin Water in 2007.

< 124 >

Also healing, miracles, the presences of spirits and beings once living now gone into another life but who continue to intrude into our waking consciousness by, for instance, haunting people or places.

Wait, we're talking about vodka, aren't we?

The implicit potential indestructibility of the soul must concern us. All of the foregoing are actual elements in our existence. Over half of the world believes in such phenomena. There are plenty of photographic and audio materials both conventional and digital and also some trace physical evidence, which support the premise that ghosts, UFOs, and their occupants, plus other nonworldly presences, exist. They indicate a supraform of reality as valid as our normal reality. But there is no jar of ectoplasm, and no one will show us the bodies from Roswell. We've had nothing to touch . . . until now.

At which point we first see the glass skull, as referenced in *Indiana Jones and the Kingdom of the Crystal Skull,* with all the mystical powers it supposedly possesses. But what's inside?

What to put in a bottle laden with such symbology and iconographic value? Such a symbol, which speaks to our own common universality, should have joy associated with it, shouldn't it? Also, since we are challenging traditional belief with the legend, the project should have a challenging aspect to it as well. We have this mystic symbol, in which we

< 125 >

have chosen to enclose joy in the form of a very pure alcoholic beverage. Which beverage, however? Only the most challenging arena in the legal recreational consumables industry—vodka.

He certainly got that right. With possibly the exception of P. Diddy, there may be no other celebrity as knowledgeable of the spirits industry as Dr. Detroit. More than three million cases of Crystal Head have sold since 2008.

It's a beautiful vessel, designed, Aykroyd explains, "by my friend, renowned American portraitist and landscape painter John Alexander, whose most recent exhibitions include showings at the American Wing of the Smithsonian Institution in Washington, DC, and at the Houston Museum of Fine Art in Houston, Texas." Warhol et al. aside, why would a serious artist engage in such a marketing ploy?

I went to find out. It was early afternoon in March, tourists thronging Broadway.

A narrow elevator—some might say a claustrophobic death trap—leads to John Alexander's SoHo studio. The enormous space has wood floors, high ceilings, and works of art on every wall. In a golf shirt, jeans, and a paint-splattered smock, Alexander came out to give me a warm welcome. He was taking a break, but this wasn't only his studio. It's also where he, his wife, son, and two dogs live.

Man with a plan (and a skull): Dan Aykroyd and Crystal Head Vodka.
Photo by Ho Yin Siu

< 127 >

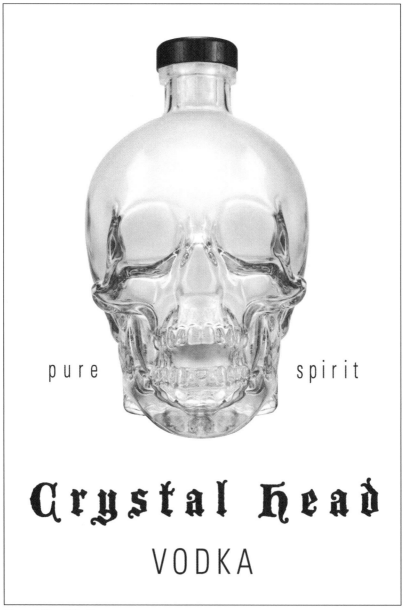

pure   spirit

𝕮𝖗𝖞𝖘𝖙𝖆𝖑 𝕳𝖊𝖆𝖉

VODKA

Crystal Head Vodka.
Courtesy of Crystal Head

John Alexander in front of Lost Souls. *Courtesy of John Alexander*

The neighborhood was a different place when he came here in 1980. It was still affordable and still highly dangerous. Alexander also had to move about quietly because at the time he could only work here, not live. Now he's sitting on a gold mine. Few other artists remain—most priced out over the years.

Alexander met Aykroyd through Bill Murray. He met Murray through a mutual friend, who owned a minor league baseball team in Texas, the artist's home state. "Murray came down on his way to *Saturday Night Live*," Alexander remembers. "He drove cross-country and stopped in Texas and ended up sleeping on my couch for a couple of weeks, and we became fast friends." Then Alexander visited the set of *SNL*. "I just fell madly in love with that whole group." Alexander doesn't see much of Murray anymore, but he and Aykroyd have remained close ever since, meeting up for birthdays, anniversaries, trips, and charitable fundraisers.

Prior to this venture the artist and actor had never engaged in a joint enterprise. In fact, all Alexander ever did was paint or, on rare occasions, sculpt. He didn't know the first thing, in Aykroyd's words, about "the most challenging arena in the legal recreational consumables industry—vodka." But he'd been thinking about it for some time.

"I use skulls in my work a lot," Alexander points out. "I think a lot of it has to do with growing up in Texas and seeing the imagery of Mexican art, and I've always loved primitive art, primitive imagery. I've always been fascinated by the art of antiquity, the kind of spiritual connotation of it. I never thought of it—and still don't—in terms of it being a symbol of death. I have more in the past than now, but you'll find depictions of

< 130 >

Heroes Come and Heroes Go (2008). *Courtesy of John Alexander*

skulls in work of mine going back to the '70s." Alexander also credits one of his teachers at Lamar University "who had us draw from the plaster cast . . . for countless, countless hours,

< 131 >

Even before Crystal Head Vodka, skulls figured prominently in the works of John Alexander. *Courtesy of John Alexander*

tedious. He was an extraordinarily gifted teacher, but he was very much in the tradition of old French and European academies where you studied the human form and the human figure and really worked tirelessly from the human skeleton, and especially a lot of skulls." In any event, "the idea just popped into my head one day to use that as a vessel for an alcoholic beverage. Everybody said it was a ridiculous idea, so I never thought about it again for ten or so years."

Aykroyd, on the other hand, knew the business extremely well. When his friend John Paul DeJoria of Paul Mitchell Hair Systems fame introduced him to Patrón tequila, the actor loved it. When Aykroyd realized Patrón wasn't available back home in Canada, he took charge of its distribution and later became involved in wines as well.

In early 2007 Alexander and Aykroyd met for lunch at Aquagrill on Spring Street and Broadway. The artist remembers eating oysters while listening to the actor discuss his thriving distribution business. "I said, 'God, that's interesting. I had an idea years ago to get into the liquor business. I wanted to do it in this skull-shaped bottle.'" Aykroyd was immediately intrigued.

"What?!" he said. "Draw it for me!"

Alexander made a rough sketch on a cocktail napkin, and Aykroyd loved it. "The next morning he comes down here [to the studio]. I do a drawing, very informal, the front and side. He takes it to Canada and shows it to these liquor distributors. I thought it would die right there because I thought, *When they see this, they're going to think we're crazy.*" On the contrary, Aykroyd's colleagues also loved it. "I was like, 'Oh no,'" Alexander recalls. "We're actually going to do this."

< 133 >

Needless to say, the experience for the Texas painter has proved overwhelming. "The first year we were in business, if I had to hear the term 'social media' one more time, I think I was going to open the window and jump out of whatever building we were in." The skull took six to eight months to go from the cocktail napkin to a physical prototype. Computers did much of the calibrating, but the real trick came down to adjusting its volume from the 750 milliliters per U.S. law to the 740 milliliters required in Great Britain. (They added half an inch more glass to the base.)

Jonathan Hemi, president of Wine Classics International, which oversees distribution of Crystal Head, told Canada's *Financial Post* that Aykroyd is "one of the hardest working people I know. He does whatever it takes to be a success and does more than many other brand owners do in his position." He adds, "Celebrity or no celebrity, I would want him as a business partner." But of course it helps enormously that he is a celebrity. Not every new vodka can organize a massive launch campaign at every House of Blues across the country. "We did Miami, Orlando, New Orleans, Houston, Dallas, Las Vegas, in that order," says Alexander. "By the time we got to Las Vegas or Dallas, we were out of product. It just went like a rocket." To date, Aykroyd has made over a hundred appearances and done countless signings on behalf of his vodka.

Taking pages from the playbooks of Ketel and Grey Goose, the team behind Crystal Head has focused on becoming the bartender's favorite. "If you're going to make a mixed drink," says Alexander, "you want to start with a clean slate. If you have a pure vodka that's not filled with citrus oils and sugars, etc., then whatever you put in it, you have a clean canvas

< 134 >

to start with, and then you can make your drink even better because you're starting with a clean product." As Aykroyd told *Bloomberg Surveillance:* "What we have here is a luxury premium spirit that has no additives. Many lesser vodkas add glycol, which is antifreeze. They add citrus oil, limonene, which is a caustic bug exterminant, and they also add sugar."

The marketing lingo reads as heavy as the promotional video, which has racked up more than three hundred thousand views on YouTube. According to the brand's website: "Pristine water from Newfoundland is blended with high quality peaches 'n' cream corn and distilled the perfect amount to preserve the natural flavour. The vodka is filtered multiple times and as a final stage passes three times through Herkimer diamonds, spiritually charged semi-precious quartz crystals."

Crystal Head Vodka is filtered through Herkimer diamond crystals.
Courtesy of Crystal Head Vodka

The challenge, however, lies not in convincing bartenders that Crystal Head is pure but rather that it can be a go-to vodka. As Ketel One's Bob Nolet said, "I would like to have one in my back bar, but I'm not going to use it. It just looks cool. But that's also what they decided to go for. If you do a skull, then you end up being an item that everybody wants but once. It's difficult to crack that."

That reaction drives John Alexander crazy. "We have to go and say, 'Wait a minute! Drink it! Come back and get a second bottle.'" He also points to the issue of depletion: "You can sell all you want, but, if you're not buying them again and depleting that product, you're dead. Early on we were having a depletions problem because we'd go out to a city, let's say Dallas, and the big liquor chain, they sell everything they've got, but six months later they're not reordering. What you had to do is convince people that there's something inside that bottle."

They also had to address the issue of handling the bottle. "Bartenders incorrectly claim that it's difficult to pour from," says Alexander. "They're used to grabbing the bottle [by the neck]. But that's okay. We're overcoming all those things."

So how exactly do you hold it, at the base or on the sides? The answer is the sides. Aykroyd has gone to bars to demonstrate proper handling, which sounds absurd, but, if Dan Aykroyd comes to your bar, you'd probably pay attention.[22]

Regardless of the challenges that Crystal Head faces, it is selling. When it launched in 2008, Aykroyd received

22 Don't store your skull in the freezer, though. Once it starts to thaw, it becomes awfully slippery no matter how you hold it.

< 136 >

permission from his three daughters to take their college funds and invest them in the vodka. He has since paid them back—and then some. His oldest daughter graduated from Harvard, her tuition paid in full. In 2011 Crystal Head Vodka won Double Gold at the San Francisco World Spirits Competition, the same title awarded to Tito's ten years earlier. Then it won a gold medal at the Moscow ProdExpo International Tasting Contest. "We're not even *in* Russia!" Alexander excitedly points out. "Our European distributor from London, he enters us in the contest, and we won it."

The March 9, 2013, episode of *Saturday Night Live* notably reassembled the Five Timers Club during Justin Timberlake's monologue. Fellow club members Alec Baldwin, Candice Bergen, Chevy Chase, Paul Simon, Steve Martin, and Tom Hanks join the newly inducted host. Playing the role of the obsequious bartender was Dan Aykroyd who, Martin notes with false pity, hosted *SNL* only once. Behind Aykroyd on the bar's top shelf stand four unmistakable bottles of Crystal Head Vodka.

But making the most of the celebrity vodka endorsement means time and commitment beyond just autograph signing and ribbon cutting. In the *Financial Post,* Aykroyd also offered this advice:

> *My best lesson so far is that you must carefully and extensively appraise the characters of the individuals with whom you anticipate placing your trust in both partnerships and in executive choices. At the first sign from someone of an undermining attitude which might indicate a coming pattern of disharmony and acrimony, a change must be made quickly. The irritation must not be left to infect everyone in*

< 137 >

the organization. The consequence for your business could be dire otherwise.

Hopefully Bill Murray, who now endorses Slovenia Vodka, and Shaquille O'Neal, who is launching his own Luv Shaq Vodka, will keep these words of wisdom in mind.[23]

---

23 Both true.

< 138 >

10

LAS VEGAS

I consider my vodka a liquid form of art.
———ASPIRING VODKA ENTREPRENEUR AT THE
NIGHTCLUB & BAR CONVENTION & TRADESHOW

So let's say you're Shaquille O'Neal and you've got a new line of vodka. Where's the best place to launch it? The answer is no longer San Francisco, as it was for Ketel One and SKYY. No, the new launch pad for new vodkas is Las Vegas during the annual Nightclub & Bar Convention & Tradeshow (NCB).

Here the makers and sellers of booze come together over free samples. If you own a bar and want to know what's new, this show is for you. Likewise, if you're a distiller and want clubs and bars to carry your brand, this show is for you. Past attendees have described the NCB as "a giant orgy," "a drunken pornfest," and "the Disneyland of bar and nightlife."

As it turns out, the debauched atmosphere apparently had to do with the NCB sharing space with an adult entertainment conference that year. But these two groups haven't met inside the Las Vegas Convention Center for a while. When

< 139 >

The Strip.
Courtesy of the Library of Congress

I paid a visit, the only neighboring confab was Pizza Expo 2013. But it's not just that. The overall atmosphere within the convention has grown tame. A dress code now applies: "Attendees should avoid wearing any clothing that may be interpreted as promiscuous, provocative, or overly sugges- tive." A code of conduct stipulates that "show management may revoke without refund the privilege of any exhibitor or attendee to attend the show or affiliated events if such exhib- itor or attendee participates in any promiscuous, sexually provocative or other inappropriate behavior as determined in the sole judgment of show management." In other words, good luck finding that drunken pornfest.

< 140 >

Behind those warnings, Jon Taffer, head of Taffer Dynamics and president of the Nightclub & Bar Media Group, probably gave death stares and barked at incompetent underlings to clean up their acts and give the convention some class. It's easy to imagine him doing that because on his hit show on Spike TV, *Bar Rescue,* it's exactly what he does.

The bar equivalent of Gordon Ramsay's *Kitchen Nightmares, Bar Rescue* focuses on flailing drinking establishments that allow Taffer to come in and shake things up. There's yelling and screaming and the occasional tossing of chairs. On one episode Taffer (rightly) berates a cook for handling raw chicken and cooked food without washing her hands:

Jon: "Tammy, I've watched you pick up raw chicken all night in your hand and then touch cooked food! [He grabs a handful of tortilla chips and throws them on the table.] Do you know how bad that is?!"

Tammy: "What the hell do I do?"

Jon: "How dare *you pick up raw chicken and then pick up cheese with your hand, pick up crab with your hand, pick up spices with your hand! Shame on you! I have never seen anything like this before! How many times have you picked up raw chicken?! Have you ever washed your hands?!"*

Tammy: "Yes."

Jon: "I'm fucking beside myself! Take that food, throw it away! Throw it all away! Shut it down! Nobody eats!"

< 141 >

Jon Taffer, the host of *Bar Rescue* and president of the Nightclub & Bar Media Group. *Courtesy of Spike TV/*Bar Rescue

But the towering host couldn't have been nicer when we met. Still intense, he doesn't mind getting up close, giving your arm a squeeze, and looking you straight in the eye.[24]

I call him a fixer, and he agrees. "But fixing the business is actually easy," he explains. "It's fixing the person that's the problem, and, if I have an approach to this that's hard, here's why. I believe that, if I tell somebody, 'Don't do this, do that. Don't do that, do this,' when I leave they go back to what

---

24 I can't prove it, but I'm not sure I ever saw him blink.

< 142 >

they used to do. I've got to change the way you think, and to change the way you think I've got to shatter the way you think now to open your brain. That's ugly. You're going to kick your heels in, you're going to push back, you're going to scream and yell. A lot of people don't like it."[25]

As for the convention, Taffer chalks it all up to exposure. "We reach 180,000 bars, and, when a new product emerges, through that show I have the ability to get it on the back bars of America," he says as he snaps his fingers. "They go home and buy it the next week, hundreds of thousands of cases of these new and emerging products. Then, once we get in on the back bar, the challenge is: How do I get people to pour it? That's where our mixology newsletters come into play and all of our mixology competitions and all the things that we do. . . . Our tradeshow side works with the actual brand ambassadors, the companies themselves, so we understand the needs and relationship of both."

Needless to say, the hit show has turned Taffer into something of a celebrity, and within the industry he's nothing short of a rock star. "Dude, it's Jon Taffer! Dude, it's Jon Taffer!" one attendee excitedly tells his friend. Dan Aykroyd came here to roll out Crystal Head a few years back. Mike "The Situation" Sorrentino did the same prior to his split with Devotion Vodka. Now CeeLo Green is scheduled to cut the ribbon

---

25 Taffer explains what these lagging businesses have in common: "When you talk to that failing manager, the common denominator is excuses. 'Oh, the economy! Oh, I have a new competitor! Oh, prices! Oh, my costs are too high! The new tax!' It's always an excuse. It's never looking at me and saying, 'Jon, I'm failing because of me.'"

< 143 >

and promote his Ty-Ku line of sake and Asian spirits. But the singer, producer, and star of *The Voice* is running late. Suddenly, from the loudspeakers, come the opening beats of "Crazy," CeeLo Green's hit song from his Gnarls Barkley days.

There's little space left near the entrance to the convention floor as the crowd waits for the star's arrival, but the song ends with still no sign of Green. The song begins again—and ends. It plays about seven times, driving everyone crazy. When Jon Taffer appears, fans yell, "Rescue us, Jon!" A few moments later Green arrives, riding a shuttle cart as if it were a Roman chariot. Short but wide, he looks comfortable in a billowy black track suit with bright red stripes.

"Welcome, everybody. Let's go! You ready?" asks the man of the hour before he cleanly snips the red ribbon. In practically one breath, Taffer quickly adds, "Thank you, CeeLo! His show here in Las Vegas, Loberace, don't miss it this month, and of course Ty-Ku, his product. You gotta try it. His booth is setting up on the floor over there now. CeeLo is going to be in the booth in a little while to say hi to you. Make sure you try it. I did. It's awesome!"

The air hums with business, but two booths appear to be less about business and more about pleasure. TurboTap USA runs the first, cosponsored by the Sapphire Pool & Dayclub. Exotic dancers are pole-dancing by the entrance, and, inside, a cheery buxom stripper offers wireless headphones.

CeeLo Green and Jon Taffer at the Nightclub & Bar Convention & Tradeshow. *STARPICZ / Splash News/Newscom*

< 144 >

She and I are listening to the same music, apparently. But what are they selling? The second booth is a lot more blatant: Larry Flynt's Hustler Club, offering discounts and free pens. A serious-looking dancer keeps repeating the same moves over and over, always culminating in a booty-clap.

Oh, and there is vodka, too. New spirits take up practically an entire aisle, most of them of the neutral grain variety. V-One Vodka—the V stands for Valley—is distilled in Poland and owned by a young man from Massachusetts named Paul Kozub. He inherited $7,000 after his grandfather, a former moonshiner, died. "I wasn't a good enough baseball player or golfer, and I'm like, I was really into vodka, so I'm going to take this money and honor him and start a business," Paul explains. The vodka has a pleasant hint of vanilla, but that ingredient also confers a brownish tint to the liquid, so the bottle isn't glass but metal. Kozub seems content with growing volume in the New England market, but having a distillery in Poland, some four thousand miles away, might prove problematic.[26]

Pool Vodka is based in New York, but founder Brian O'Reilly hopes it becomes the spirit of choice in the warmer climes of Miami and Southern California. "It's six times distilled, from

---

[26] It also seemed impolitic to point out that it shares a name with the infamous German rocket from World War II.

Pool Vodka. Turn the bottle upside down and the label still reads "Pool."
Courtesy of BevKo, LLC

< 146 >

Global Vodka: European grain distilled in Italy into vodka by an Armenian and sold in America. *Courtesy of Global Vodka*

wheat, and then six times carbon filtered, which takes out any trace of an impurity that could possibly be in the vodka," he assures. Its motto? "Get in. Get wet." Forget about having a Sex on the Beach; with Pool you can have a Sex in the Pool! The logo is an ambigram: It reads "Pool" right side up and upside down.

According to Chanel Turner, CEO and owner of Fou-Dré, the vodka market is stale and lacking in innovative bottle designs. "It's a round, clear bottle—that's most vodkas across the market," she observes. This explains why her Fou-Dré—French for lightning—comes in a purple glass container shaped like a lightning bolt. "We have a patented distillation

< 148 >

method called the TerrePure process—basically it removes all the free radicals and gives it a very neat and clean finish."

Meanwhile, Global Vodka is one of the few vodkas distilled in Italy, although owner Levon Mgrdichian (not Italian) points out the grains are European. Inna Feldman-Gerber of Premiere Distillery claims her Real Russian Vodka is "the only American vodka crafted by real Russians"—whatever that means.

From San Antonio, Texas, Nicholas Spink, founder of Spike Vodka, says, "I wanted something unique. I didn't want to be one of these mass brand, potato or corn or what have you, or an NGS. I could've taken the easy way out. So I researched something that hasn't been done." He elaborates: "Vodka in Russia was made with potatoes because there was an over-supply of an item.[27] In the Midwest it's corn because you've got all this corn. In Texas we have an overabundance of cactus. So I started experimenting and doing a lot of research, and it took over four and a half years to create my product"—a vodka distilled from cactus. "We're the first and only one in the world."

It's an intriguing taste, almost like tequila, though Spink quickly points out that the agave plant and cactus don't come from the same family. Then Spink reveals something else that makes Spike unique: "We're the only gay owned and operated vodka company. There're other vodka companies that are owned by gays, but we're gay owned and operated. Everybody who works for Spike is gay." Sure they only have four employees, but it's still one hell of a selling point.

---

27 Most Russian vodkas are grain-based.

< 149 >

By late afternoon my head is spinning, either from all the sampling or from hearing too often how many times a vodka has been distilled and carbon filtered. Maybe it was the vodka with the LED light at the base of the bottle that sent me over the edge. Click a button once, and it glows; click it twice, and it blinks. Meanwhile, the rest of Sin City is gearing up for another long night of drinking.

To get a sense of just how much booze Las Vegas consumes, I visited the regional offices of Southern Wine & Spirits, the country's largest distributor of alcohol. The Vegas operation is massive, taking up 340,000 square feet. The assistant warehouse operations manager, John Madden—who looks not at all like that John Madden but rather L.A. Clippers forward Blake Griffin—takes me for a ride in a shuttle cart, which he calls his Cadillac. We cruise through chilly air down long corridors stacked sky-high with every brand imaginable. The warehouse was meant to house 850,000 cases, explains Madden, but capacity has reached well over 1 million and looks like the warehouse scene at the end of *Raiders of the Lost Ark.*

No area is brand-specific. Workers stock wherever there's space. Madden likens it to a game of Tetris. Each case bears a receiving sticker, which is scanned and can be electronically located in one of 16,500 different locations. Southern does everything: liquor, wine, beer, energy drinks, bottled water.

John Madden, assistant warehouse operations manager at Southern Wine & Spirits, Las Vegas. *Courtesy of John Madden*

< 150 >

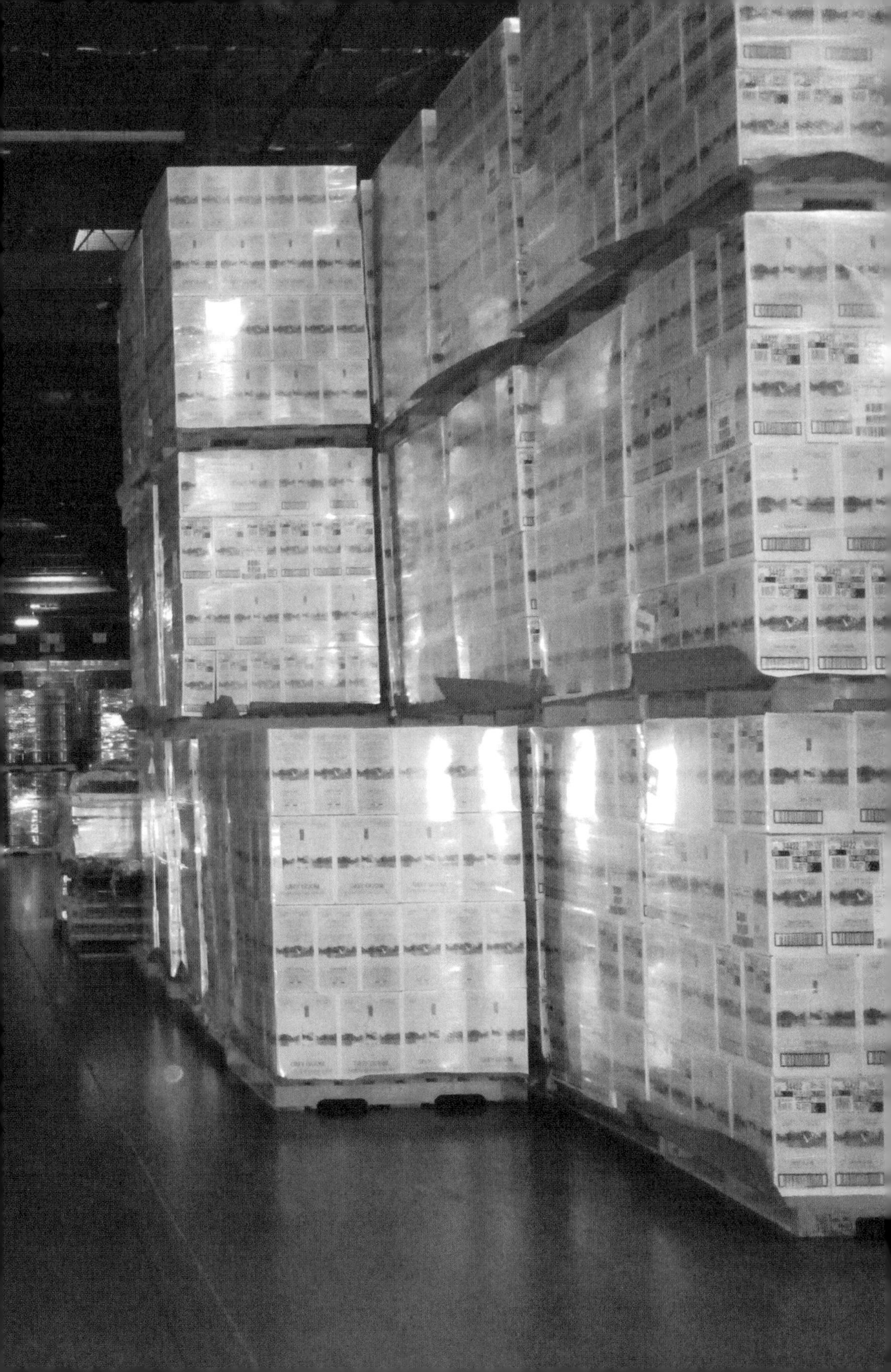

But alcohol pays the bills here. The most popular beer in Las Vegas, at least based on the activities at Southern, is Corona. They move about five thousand cases a night. As for liquor, no surprise that it's vodka, primarily Grey Goose. "Absolutely," says John, who notes that this facility supplies 3,500 accounts.

With so much product on the move, the workers take care to avoid collisions. Getting hit by a forklift isn't pretty. At every turn a driver must honk his horn. The entire place constantly echoes with horns. We pass the seemingly endless Grey Goose corridor and come upon a section closed off by a chain-link fence. It houses some of the pricier products, including Melchizideks (thirty-liter bottles) of Armand de Brignac's Ace of Spades champagne, which can retail as high as $50,000. It is also a Jay-Z favorite since he boycotted Roederer Cristal. Even more outrageous is the crate containing a thirty-liter bottle of Boerl & Kroff champagne, which can run $89,000 at a club.

"It's a great place to work," Madden says with a big smile. I believe him, though I'd much rather have the job of Francesco Lafranconi, Southern Wine & Spirits's executive director of mixology and spirits education. The amiable Italian, who has worked in four-star establishments in Gleneagles, Bolzano, and Gstaad, now educates the bartenders of Las

Like the final scene from "Raiders of the Lost Ark"—The cavernous warehouse of Southern Wine & Spirits in Las Vegas. *Courtesy of John Madden*

< 154 >

Francesco Lafranconi, head mixologist at Southern Wine & Spirits of Nevada.
Courtesy of Francesco Lafranconi

Vegas at Southern's in-house Academy of Spirits and Fine Service.[28]

As Francesco explained in a 2010 issue of the *Tasting Panel,* "There is nothing more satisfying for me than to see these passionate bartenders and beverage managers committing themselves to the program, learning how products are made, acquire proper tasting techniques and terminology that will help them increase sales, and all while mixing ingredients into cocktails with remarkable balance." It must kill him to see all those drunk frat guys and girls walking down

---

28 The Southern facility also has a conference room, dining room, tasting room, and bar.

< 155 >

the Strip with their plastic bong-like containers filled with Fat Tuesday's 190 Octane special.

We stop at the bar, and he asks, "What do you like?" It's a tough question coming from one of the world's great mixologists. "Vodka? Rum? Gin? Whiskey?" He guesses vodka, to which I assent, but I note that I've been drinking gin of late. He makes something that contains Absolut Pear and Plymouth Gin called a Sorriso. "It's Italian for 'smile' because I noticed a lot of bartenders are forgetting to smile."

According to Francesco's Luxardo recipe book, the drink also contains sherry, cherry brandy, "Sangue Morlacco" liqueur, and bitters. He pours it into a martini glass with a macerated cherry and just a hint of orange and lemon from the peels. It's no orgy, but it's delicious.

< 156 >

11

FLAVOR COUNTRY

The largest liquor companies in the world haven't launched more than five hundred flavored vodkas because no one wanted to drink them.

—Jason Wilson, *Boozehound*

Few outside the industry realize that Beam Global—with annual sales approaching $3 billion and thirty-four million cases worldwide—owns not only iconic brown spirits like Maker's Mark, Knob Creek, and the eponymous Jim Beam, but also Effen, Kamchatka, Pinnacle, and Vox vodkas. The company's second best-selling product, right behind Jim Beam whiskey, is Pinnacle with close to three million cases per year.

To some, especially craft distillers, Pinnacle has become an abomination, and its sin has ensured its success. Pinnacle, which brands itself a French vodka but is distilled in Lewiston, Maine, offers thirty flavors. They include Blueberry, Cake, Cherry Lemonade, Cherry Whipped, Chocolate Whipped, Cookie Dough, Cotton Candy, Le Double Espresso, Gummy, Kiwi-Strawberry, Mango, Marshmallow, Orange, Orange

< 157 >

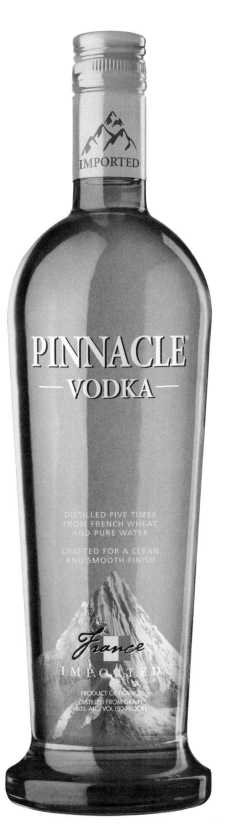

Pinnacle Vodka,
the original.
Courtesy of Beam Inc.

Pinnacle Blue Martini,
also known as Island
Disco at Dusk.
Courtesy of Beam Inc.

Have your cake and eat it, too—a Pinnacle Birthday Cake cocktail using Cake-flavored Pinnacle Vodka. *Courtesy of Beam Inc.*

Whipped, Red Berry, Swedish Fish, Tropical Punch, Vanilla, and—the most popular—Whipped. It's a far cry from the subtly sweet and delicately nuanced Sorriso that Francesco Lafranconi made in Las Vegas.

Others have followed suit. Van Gogh makes a vodka that tastes like peanut butter and jelly. Oddka, a subdivision of Wyborowa, owned by Pernod Ricard, showcases such flavors as Apple Pie, Electricity, Fresh Cut Grass, Salty Caramel Popcorn, and Wasabi. Who knew electricity had flavor?[29] Even Diageo has gotten in on the action with Smirnoff flavors Fluffed Marshmallow and Whipped Cream. Diageo ran a commercial for them, in which a female voice says, "I might choose Fluffed. Then again, I might choose Whipped. Either way, vodka never felt this good." As Stuart Elliott of the *New York Times* points out, "Yes, those are shorthand ways to say the names of the two new flavors. But each of those words also has a meaning that is not so easily discussed in a blog from a family newspaper."

Not everyone is joining the parade. To date, Ketel One offers a mere two flavors, Citroen and Oranje—and they weren't even the Nolets' idea. "In 2000 we came out with Ketel Citroen because the bartenders were asking us, 'Please, please, get us Ketel One–based citron because we're now using another product from the north of Europe and it's actually not the right base for our cosmo,'" Bob Nolet recalls. In California Carolus happened upon a grocery store customer

---

29 And what poor soul did the testing to find out what it was?

< 161 >

Grey Goose La Poire; Grey Goose Le Citron; Grey Goose L'Orange; Grey Goose Cherry Noir. *Courtesy of Grey Goose*

Ketel One Citroen.
Courtesy of the Nolet Distillery

carrying a bottle of Ketel and another flavored brand. The shopper explained that he was making martinis and cosmos for a party and "if Ketel One had a citron, I would buy Ketel One." At which point Carolus revealed himself and promised to make it happen. Otherwise, Bob says, "less is better" because "we're not a flavored vodka, we're Ketel One Vodka."[30]

"It's certainly where the business is going," Dan Aykroyd told *Bloomberg Surveillance*. "But I always like to say about our vodka, I'm in the vodka-flavored vodka business." Tito Beveridge draws a similar line. "We're not doing any other flavors—we're doing 80 proof vodka, that's it. We do one thing and try to do it right," he says. "You go look at the vodka section, and there are Froot Loops and Gummi Bears and every flavor, Jolly Ranchers, anything you

---

30 But nothing's stopping them from introducing a Ketel jenever in a couple of decades.

< 164 >

An ad for Pinnacle Whipped Vodka with innocent images but a suggestive tagline.
Courtesy of Beam Inc.

ate as a kid, SweeTarts, any kind of cereal, whipped cream, brownies, fudge, caramel, cotton candy, cupcakes."

Pinnacle's latest flavors include Rainbow Sherbet and Cinnabon. That's right—Cinnabon.

Renowned mixologist Derek Brown says the flavors are trying to appeal to a nostalgia for childhood. The problem, he wrote in the *Atlantic Monthly* in 2012, is that "nostalgically flavored vodkas are more likely to apply a literal interpretation of flavor. Whipped cream vodka tastes like, well, whipped cream vodka, which mostly tastes like whipped cream." His point is that "while cocktails and spirits may express a diversity of flavors and levels of complexity, those that sit at the bottom rung for me are those that express very little complexity and seek to deliver the package (intoxication) without asking for the toll. Alcoholic beverages shouldn't necessarily taste good to both children and pets."

Brown's criticism falls on deaf ears. According to the Distilled Spirits Council of the United States, 21 percent of all vodkas sold in 2012 were flavored, and the entire category grew by 19 percent. Beam Global couldn't be happier.

The largest U.S.–based spirits company resides within a massive stone-gray building in an office park in Deerfield, northwest of Chicago, across the street from its former owner, Fortune Brands.[31] A lounge and bar in the lobby features every Beam brand, well, beaming from the shelves. On

---

[31] At one point, Fortune owned Beam, Moen Faucets, Titleist, and Footjoy, among other assorted products. In January 2014 it was announced that Japanese beverage giant Suntory would acquire Beam for $13.6 billion.

< 166 >

the third floor, past a sea of cubicles, I meet with John Horn in the conference room. His official title is director of field marketing in control states.[32] But Horn, a solid-looking guy in his mid-forties, knows Beam history and industry trends. He helped launch Effen Vodka.

Beam has a vodka for every price point, from value-brand Kamchatka to top-shelf Vox and Effen. "It's definitely part of a strategy," he admits. It's no different than managing a well-balanced stock portfolio. When one fund sinks, another hopefully rises.

Kamchatka retails for $8.99. But every time I mention the brand, Horn laughs nervously, as if I'm referring to an illegitimate child. "It's a very regional brand. It's not prolific over every geography in the United States. There are markets like Ohio where it is actually the number one spirit consumed in the state," he says with a laugh. It's true—NPR even did a story on it. In 2010 Ohioans consumed four hundred thousand gallons of Kamchatka, and it now comes in flavors. "They're going well—surprisingly well, because I didn't think that a person who picked that price point would want a flavor option, but they do."[33]

How many states carry Kamchatka?

"Oof. I don't know off the top of my head," Horn says. It seems he *doesn't* want to know. "It's a viable brand in a viable category. If consumers didn't want it, it wouldn't exist." For

---

32 In eighteen states, the state governments control liquor stores and sales.

33 The bottle also made a cameo on *Mad Men* on Don Draper's bar cart along with Canadian Club Whiskey, another Beam product.

< 167 >

the record, Americans spent $1.1 billion on value-brand vodkas in 2012, compared with $1.3 billion for super-premiums.

On the other hand, Horn happily discusses Beam's acquisition of Skinnygirl, a line of low-calorie ready-to-serve drinks—no mixing necessary—created by Bethenny Frankel, a reality TV star, natural foods chef, and talk show host. Frankel built her brand with the help of David Kanbar, nephew of SKYY inventor Maurice Kanbar. She started with bottles of margarita, and Beam has brought out Skinnygirl Mojito, Moscato, and White Cherry Vodka with Natural Flavors. According to Horn the latter has 20 percent fewer calories than other vodkas, roughly seventy-seven calories per serving. "It fits a lifestyle of women, not only Bethenny fans," he explains, but also the "calorie conscious."

Of course the former Real Housewife of New York gets the last laugh. Beam paid her a considerable but undisclosed sum for her product, one that many had turned down when she wanted to sell. "There's a number out there," says Horn, but "you're not going to want to put that in the book because it's in a double-digit multiple of what was actually paid for it." The "number out there" is $100 million. But even if that figure were accurate, the investment is already paying off. Annual volume for Skinnygirl is approaching a million cases.

Horn knows the criticisms of flavored vodka. But Pinnacle sells in the millions of cases. "Not every vodka brand is like that or for that," he says, trying to be diplomatic. "I am sure you've spoken to many that can't get outside of the basic citrus, pear, cherry, and those types of things. It just doesn't fit their profile." He also suggests more flavors will

< 168 >

come. "Flavored vodka is really a microcosm of what goes on with any type of flavor. There are generations coming up and drinking spirits who had more choices than anybody else in any generation before them when it came to flavors. . . . Soda companies are making machines where you just pick your own flavors. They're all competing with one another for that. Tastes change, and tastes and flavors evolve."

Horn is right. The trend reflects the broadening of flavors in many other product realms as well. As John Jeffery, master craft distiller at Death's Door in Wisconsin, points out, "The next time you're in the grocery store, look at how many chewing gum flavors there are. When you were a kid it was Doublemint and Juicy Fruit. Now there's forty-five different flavors of gum, all from the same companies because they're just looking to fill up shelves. It's the same phenomenon with toothpaste. It's the natural progression of the affluent growth of the 1990s and this disposable income, and here are all your choices and head off to the party."[34]

Jeffery's colleague at Death's Door, founder Brian Ellison, sees a logic to the trend. "I always think of the flavored vodka market as female, sort of twenty-one to twenty-nine, and she's walking into a liquor store and being like, 'I'm going to a party. I'm either going to buy a bottle of wine,

---

[34] Add lollipops to the list. Gourmet company Lollyphile sent out press releases touting its latest concoction, the breast milk lollipop. "What slowly dawned on me," says owner Jason Darling, "was that my friends were actually producing milk so delicious it could turn a screaming, furious child into a docile, contented one. I knew I had to capture that flavor."

< 169 >

or I'm going to buy two six-packs of beer, or for the same price I could buy a really interesting bottle of flavored vodka that I can bring that's fun, that I can mix something in it.' It's unique."[35]

Absolut debuted Peppar in 1986 and Citron two years later, which started the current trend, but flavors, and particularly infusions, go back at least two centuries. In the Russian Samovar in midtown Manhattan, owner Roman Kaplan has a photocopied manuscript dated 1802 detailing vodka infusions. The restaurant does a wide variety of its own, including coriander, dill, garlic, horseradish, peach, and pineapple, and you can see the infusion jars behind the bar.

"My main concern was to have a drink that also helps you with this or that disease. That was the basic idea, to give people drinks infused," Roman says in his thick Russian accent. "For example," he reads from an Internet printout, "cranberries are good for colds, they increase one's energy, help cure and heal infections in the urinary tract, help prevent prostate cancer, and enriched with many different vitamins."

Before coming to America in 1977, Roman was a literature professor and learned English by reading *Great Expectations.* He opened the Russian Samovar in 1986 with the help of the late poet Joseph Brodsky and Mikhail Baryshnikov. Roman

---

35 Nevertheless, Ellison says the search for more vodka flavors reminds him of the *Onion* headline: "Pornography-Desensitized Populace Demands New Orifice to Look at." "That's really what it feels like," he says. "It's like, well, we did whipped. Now let's do chocolate whipped! Now let's do caramel whipped!"

< 170 >

has a cameo in an episode of *Sex and the City* thanks to the famous dancer, who played Carrie Bradshaw's boyfriend. One night, while visiting the Samovar, Baryshnikov went out for a smoke with Roman. A group of tourists walked by and, according to the owner, one of them pointed at the ballet legend and yelled out, "That's the artist guy from *Sex and the City!*" The artist guy didn't appreciate it.

In any event, the infusing process takes about ten days, and they use Russian Standard vodka. Bartender Vlad says they once tried to do bacon-infused vodka, but the result was disastrous: It had a texture akin to bacon grease.

Until recently, vodka flavors remained focused on fruits and spices. Think Absolut Peppar, Citron, and Kurant and Stoli Ohranj and Citros. But then the trend shifted.

"It's what I call 'jumping species,'" says Maura McGinn of SKYY. "Before it was, How do you make a drink? You put a lemon twist in there. Well, suddenly there's an easy way to make a cocktail at home by having a citrus-flavored vodka. But the thing is, when you get into things like whipped cream or whatever, that's a food. People are going to say, 'Oh, I'm going to make a dessert—I eat a Tiramisu, suddenly I want a Tiramisu vodka.'" The notion of flavors emulating foods brings to mind the full-course meal chewing gum from Roald Dahl's *Charlie and the Chocolate Factory:* "This piece of gum I've just made happens to be tomato soup, roast beef, and blueberry pie, but you can have almost anything you want!"

Well, almost anything. Toward the end of my interview, I ask Horn how often people come to him with flavor suggestions. "I get this all the time," he says. He's heard everything

< 171 >

from scrambled eggs and bacon to maple wood and cedar. He leans back in his chair, ready to hear my own suggestion.

Breast milk.

"Oof," he says, as if punched in the gut. "That's not where I thought you were going to go with that one."

The weirdest flavor suggestion he's ever heard?

"Breast milk. You just took the cake. That is now the weirdest I've heard."

Joking aside, can the flavor category get any bigger? Pinnacle has started to rotate flavors in and out, sometimes depending on the season, with Pumpkin Pie a huge success in the fall. "We look at trends. We look at where consumers' tastes are going . . . We have a complete, multimillion-dollar R&D center down in Kentucky that does nothing but employ the best-in-class people who work on flavors and consumer insights and everything else."

But Horn does see a scaling back in the industry. "I don't think you need fifteen of one flavor, right?[36] Vodka is the biggest category but still growing. There's a place to have expansion, but to the rate that it's going right now? I think there will eventually be a little bit of reshuffling of the deck and a little bit of a contraction."

What's the next big spirit boom?

"Selfishly, as the world's largest bourbon company, there are a lot of people saying bourbon is the next vodka, which

---

36 Derek Brown would no doubt lead the chorus yelling, "Right!"

< 172 >

doesn't make us sad," he says with a laugh. If Beam can lure more women to drink brown spirits through its Red Stag cherry- and honey-flavored bourbons—of which close to 50 percent of its drinkers already are female—this very well could happen. Horn, however, has doubts. "The place that vodka has found, the mixability of it, the approachability of it, there are a lot of things that vodkas offer that many others don't."

Either way, Beam is covered.

< 173 >

12

BACKLASH

If, therefore, you need grain alcohol to dilute your tincture of iodine or to rub on your back and the corner drug store is closed, just use vodka. Of course the vodka is half distilled water but that won't harm your back at all.
—DAVID A. EMBURY, THE FINE ART OF MIXING DRINKS
(1958 EDITION)

But there are other reasons to loathe vodka. On May 3, 2004, the *New York Observer* ran a story headlined "Bottle Boobs Buy $300 Vodka." Someone had devised a new way to jump the line. All you had to do, writes Sheelah Kolhatkar, was "wave a credit card and utter the only password that comes close to guaranteeing passage into Manhattan's inner night-life sanctum these days: 'Bottle service!'" According to Kolhatkar, the practice had deep implications:

The time-honored New York City tradition of velvet-rope profiling based on looks, coolness, and connections has given way to a cruder calculus: In the ultimate triumph of money

< 175 >

over beauty, the willingness to drop hundreds on a bottle of Absolut has become the major criterion for admittance to the city's desirable nightspots, especially for those who would otherwise be rejected for the old reasons. Like Vegas high rollers, cretinous bores with a little space left on their MasterCards rule the night—until that bottle of Grey Goose goes empty.

As for the result:

"It's symptomatic of the demise of the idea of a scene, because with bottle service anyone can get in, and that defeats the whole purpose," said Noah Kerner, who used to D.J. for Jennifer Lopez and is now a partner in a marketing company. "There's certainly no inherent connection between cool and rich. There might even be an inverse relationship. So the less space there's going to be for fun people who have good energy, people who make a room."

During the 2013 Las Vegas Nightclub & Bar Show, a welcome party took place at Hyde, a nightclub designed by Philippe Starck inside the Bellagio. Even at the seriously unfashionable hour of 9:00 p.m., a line had formed. But not all NCB attendees had received an invite, just those who opted for the extended package. Party staff gently escort one man out of line, a look of shame, embarrassment, and humiliation on his face.

Inside, the place is mobbed. The room is partly open air, and from time to time the famous Bellagio fountains perform, shooting water 460 feet into the air and gracing some with a welcome, cooling mist. Rapper Pitbull blares from the speakers.

< 176 >

But even inside, ropes separate those happy just to get in from those who reserved booths for bottle service. There are two options. If I plan on staying only until 11:30 p.m., I can reserve a booth and request one bottle for $550, but then I need to vacate once Hyde opens to its regular clubgoers. If I want to stay the whole night, I can reserve the booth for anywhere from $3,000 to $5,000. To counter the look of incredulity on my face, the manager explains that this sum counts against my booze expenses, so I can buy a few midlevel bottles that add up to the three or four grand, or I can buy one or two really expensive bottles totaling the same amount. A 1.75-liter bottle of Grey Goose, Belvedere, or Absolut runs $1,100. Gone are the days of $300 bottle service. The good news is that for the price you get free club soda, tonic, and lime wedges—not to mention those mists from the Bellagio fountains. Clearly a deal.

In the darkened club a tall fellow named Pete, who operates several lounges in Washington State, is standing nearby. He shakes his head. "The crazy thing," he says, "is the guy who ends up ordering bottle service at 1:00 a.m. is usually too drunk to drink any of it."

Is it any wonder that the vodka boom has met with backlash?

After *Food & Wine* published its *Cocktails '09* recipe book—with a marked decline in the number of libations using vodka as the base—drinks writer Eric Felten exulted in the spirit's decline. "At long last, as a revolutionary theorist might put it, the contradictions inherent in the vodka paradigm have become apparent," he wrote in the *Wall Street Journal.* "It's as though there were finally the realization that making cocktails with vodka is like making paella with instant rice—it can be

< 177 >

done, of course, but it doesn't exactly burnish one's culinary bona fides."

Felten, author of *How's Your Drink? Cocktails and the Art of Drinking Well,* says the backlash "among the best bartenders" began in 2005. That sounds about right. In 2008 the PX lounge was encouraging its patrons to try exotic concoctions like the Smoker's Delight—tobacco-infused tea, honey, bourbon, lemon juice, water—and other libations involving house-made bitters. The Alexandria, Virginia, speakeasy even had a sign on the wall warning customers *not* to order vodka tonics.

But other reasons to take issue with the neutral spirit arose. "There simply is no such thing as a vodka *martini,*" insists Jason Wilson, author of *Boozehound: On the Trail of the Rare, the Obscure, and the Overrated in Spirits.* "The martini is certainly more of a broad concept than a specific recipe, but the one constant must be gin and vermouth. Beyond correctness, vodka and vermouth is just a terrible match." The next time you go out, ask for a martini, up, with olives. A waiter worth his or her salt will ask if you want gin or vodka. When food writer Michael Ruhlman ordered one at a bar, he was asked what vodka he preferred. He walked out.

Wilson blames Ian Fleming for introducing the vodka martini to readers in *Casino Royale,* "along with the ridiculous concept of shaking and not stirring a martini. . . . A martini should always be stirred. That's the only way you can achieve that silky smooth texture and dry martini clearness. . . . A shaken martini is a weaker drink."

Cocktail historian David Embury expressed similar concerns. "There are people who like vodka martinis, but, unless

< 178 >

you use much more vermouth than I recommend, you will have nothing but raw alcohol with a faint herb flavor from the vermouth." Embury wrote this in the 1958 edition of his best-selling cocktail guide, *The Fine Art of Mixing Drinks.* It turns out that vodka-hating has been going on for some time.

Embury, "neither a distiller, an importer, a bottler, a liquor merchant, nor even a retired bartender"—according to his brave author bio—had to revise his book, originally published in 1948, to address the rise of vodka,

> *a wholly characterless, dilute grain alcohol that has streaked across the firmament of mixed drinks like Halley's Comet. As I said in the first edition, 'It makes an excellent cocktail base, and, having no pronounced flavor of its own, it will blend with anything.' On the other hand—and just because it is wholly characterless in itself—it has definite limitations. It is hard to conceive of any worse cocktail monstrosity than the Vodka Martini, the Vodka Old-Fashioned, or Vodka on Rocks.*

He also abhors the Moscow Mule, the Bloody Mary, and the Screwdriver. The spirit itself he deplores as "nothing but pure, high-proof grain alcohol and water. It is nothing but the 'Mountain Dew,' 'White Mule,' or 'Cawn Likker' (and a substantial part of it is made from corn) so well known in our own Southland, having even less character and flavor."

Embury wasn't alone. "From time to time," he writes, "my friends have said to me, 'Dave, I have been given a bottle of vodka. What the (mustn't say the naughty word) do I do with it?'" Around the same time, *New Yorker* legend A. J. Liebling let loose his own tirade against the neutral spirit.

< 179 >

"The standard of perfection for vodka (no color, no taste, no smell)," he explained,

> *was expounded to me long ago by the then Estonian consul-general in New York, and it accounts perfectly for the drink's rising popularity with those who like their alcohol in conjunction with the reassuring tastes of infancy—tomato juice, orange juice, chicken broth. It is the ideal intoxicant for the drinker who wants no reminder of how hurt Mother would be if she knew what he was doing.*

His words ring an eerily similar note to Derek Brown's observation that vodka flavors invoke our nostalgia for youth and innocence. As he jokingly put it in the *Atlantic Monthly,* "If spirits writers and apocalyptic cults are right and the world actually ends in 2012, it will be because of the new wave of flavored vodkas that evoke a stream of childhood memories." Of course the world didn't end—and more vodka flavors have debuted than ever.[37]

A few years ago Brown was running the Columbia Room, a speakeasy tucked inside his brother's bar, The Passenger,

---

37 Including Skorppio Vodka, which contains an actual and, according to the distiller, edible scorpion.

Derek Brown, not the biggest fan of vodka.
Courtesy Derek Brown/photographer Scott Suchman

< 180 >

near the DC Convention Center. Today he operates the Columbia Room, Mockingbird Hill, which specializes in sherry, a whiskey bar called Southern Efficiency, and Eat the Rich, an oyster house. His brother also runs a rum bar called Hogo. But according to *GQ,* the Columbia Room is one of the best cocktail bars in the country, and Brown one of America's best martini-makers.

"To us," he says, "the important thing is that we make a great drink, and vodka is capable of that. But it's the chicken breast of cocktails. It's the most boring, least thoughtful sort of one that you can mix with. . . . For a craft bartender—someone who believes in humanity—this stuff is just a joke and will fade away." Brown still respects customers who order vodka drinks, but his bar carries only one vodka: Boyd & Blair. He finds ways to steer them toward alternatives such as gin, which, he says, "is just flavored vodka. It just happens to be a very good flavor of vodka."

Inviting me to do a blind vodka taste test, he returns from the next-door Passenger bar a few minutes later with two sets of four tall shot glasses, each filled with room-temperature non-flavored vodka. "You do best to expectorate," Brown suggests, meaning taste but don't ingest. He would know. Brown regularly serves as a judge on spirit tastings and estimates that, over the last three months, he has sampled at least sixty different vodkas.

One shot at a time, we compare notes about purity, mouthfeel, hints of oat, banana, or citrus. Once I arranged them in order of preference, he revealed their identities. My favorite—sweet, citrusy, and with only a slight burn—was SKYY. Second came the almost minty Stolichnaya. Third was

< 182 >

an artisanal vodka called Smooth Ambler, which has hints of banana but felt a little rough around the edges. Much to my surprise, my least favorite turned out to be Ketel One, a vodka I normally choose over Stoli.

Brown says that a person's preference of drink and brand can reveal a lot. "If the person orders Grey Goose, the one thing it says, more than anything, is that he's just a follower, that he's part of the herd. If he orders something like Ketel One, then maybe he's seeking a little more level of sophistication." Brown quickly explains that he is generalizing, and of course it's not that simple. "I'm just saying you can tell the identities in these vodkas are all wrapped up in one. Each vodka tells a little about a person's personality." He also counts many of the new vodkas as scams. "Essentially charlatans are making some of the crappiest vodkas that exist, and they're putting them in different-shaped bottles with really nice-looking labels."

I tell him that I enjoy SKYY, which prompts him to ask if I studied economics in school. I did—four miserable semesters of it—which brings a smile to Brown's face. He elaborates: "The SKYY personality is somebody who is much more analytical—because it's an analysis. If you look at it, it's relatively inexpensive, but it's still a call, right?"

As much as Derek looks down on vodka, he finds himself drawn to Ketel One. "It definitely has an image like, If you're wearing a tuxedo and you want to skip the masses who are all ordering the Grey Goose, you say 'I'll take the Ketel One.' It's a classic just from the lettering to the age of Ketel One, which actually made jenever historically, which is pretty cool."

< 183 >

While on the subject of drinker profiling, I throw my friend Steve S. under the bus. Despite a taste for the finer things in life, Steve used to love drinking Stolichnaya Razberi and Sprite. (He no longer does.) He ordered it unapologetically at bars. Brown's face freezes for a second before he shakes his head. "Oh, it's embarrassing. That's like a stripper shot. . . . People don't really realize what they order says a lot about who they are and everyone around them. That's embarrassing."

So what about the Columbia Room patron who walks in and orders a vodka drink? First Derek might ask, "Do you mind flavored vodka?" which opens the way to gin. "The thing is this—not that I don't want them to be happy and order what they want, because I really do want them to be happy, but—I don't believe happiness is that cheap. At the end of the day, it's much more interesting, if you come back here, to get something you've never tried before."

He continues: "*GQ* says I make one of the best martinis in the United States, so I pass it across the bar. You go, 'I don't like this.' Then I go, 'Good, then I'll make you a vodka martini.' It's real simple, you know? At least it really shows that you probably don't like gin and you never will. But the funny thing that usually happens is that people who are ardent vodka supporters, when I make it well, using all the skill I can muster, I pass it across the bar, and they sip it, they go, 'Oh, I like this.' Well, that's what it's supposed to be, you know? That's the problem."

That said, Brown still sees a glimmer of hope thanks to the efforts of craft distillers. "They're changing the way people look at vodka: You have High West Whiskey or Oat Whiskey,

< 184 >

which is in some ways a vodka. They call it a whiskey, it's barrel-aged, but it's a neutral spirit. . . . You see people who are producing flavorful vodkas. That doesn't meet the Tax & Trade Bureau's assessment of what a vodka should be, but it certainly is what a vodka can be."

< 185 >

13

PIONEERING SPIRIT

There's nothing more American than a good Russian spirit.
—Lance Winters, master distiller and
proprietor of St. George Spirits

When the American Distilling Institute was founded in 2003, it registered just sixty-nine craft distillers. Today it records more than seven hundred. Craft distillers typically emphasize quality of product over marketing, substance over style—and certainly "lifestyle." They don't chase celebrity endorsements or sponsor Oscar afterparties. A quirky bunch, they remain earnest in their endeavors and outspoken in their beliefs.

You can find craft distillers everywhere in the country, and obviously there are too many of them to chronicle in one book. So limiting myself to a handful, aside from Koval Distillery in Chicago, I visited St. George Spirits in Alameda, California; Anchor Distilling in San Francisco; Death's Door in Middleton, Wisconsin; and Industry City Distillery in Brooklyn.

The doors of craft distillers are always open. They've got nothing to hide. Good luck trying to see the Smirnoff distillery

< 187 >

A rare look inside the Smirnoff distillery in Plainfield, Illinois.
PR NEWSWIRE/Newscom

in Plainfield, Illinois, or that of Luxco in St. Louis, makers of Tvarscki and Pearl vodkas as well as Everclear. American Harvest's operations in Idaho were also off limits probably because Distilled Resources Inc. processes their neutral grain spirits and also supplies Blue Ice, CheapShot, Ecstasy Liqueur, Famous Vodka, and Square One, among others.

Actually their doors aren't always open. Arriving an hour early for a 1:30 p.m. appointment at St. George Spirits, I find the doors locked . . . in the middle of nowhere. This used to be Alameda Naval Air Station. The 2,527-acre complex occupied a third of Alameda Island, about fifteen miles from downtown San Francisco, just across the bay. The station, with its three hundred buildings, was closed in 1997. One of those buildings, a hangar, has become home to St. George Spirits, maker of

< 188 >

absinthe, bourbon, gin, rum, and Hangar One Vodka. By the time I down a chili dog from a Mexican food truck sent from heaven, the public entrance has opened, and I meet Lance Winters, master distiller and sole proprietor of St. George Spirits.

He looks like a Bond villain. Don't get me wrong—Winters is a friendly guy with a deep, soulful voice, but he's also big, bald, with thick-framed glasses, mustache, and a goatee. He hands me his business card, which reads, "Lance Winters, Evil Genius."

His office, as expected, has a bar. Sunk into a brown leather chair, Winters guesses the idea came to him around 2000. He and his business partner, Jörg Rupf, had been making eaux de vie—not exactly a big seller. During the off season, Winters visited bars and noticed the proliferation of flavored vodkas. "Every time I would sit down to taste one, the one thing that was consistent was disappointment. They were all terrible," he remembers. "I don't want to cast aspersions on any competitors, but there would be a fruit name on the label, and that fruit would be a very distant second in both aroma and flavor to the ethanol." At which point he told Rupf: "Our eaux de vie are a hundred times more intensely flavorful than any of these things, but these are selling like hotcakes. Nobody's going to reach for an eau de vie on the shelf to make a cocktail, but everybody reaches for a flavored vodka. We should try our hands at this."

"Typically," he continues, "what people would do when they were making a flavored vodka, they'd start with a relatively clean ethanol base and then have flavors synthesized or naturally pulled from ingredients standardized and just blend those in. We like to do things the harder way. We started

< 189 >

sourcing fruit, started infusing that and redistilling it and finding that we could make very flavorful, very forward character spirits." With the help of Ansley Coale of Germain-Robin brandies, Hangar One was born. They began in 2002 with 250 cases, and sure enough they sold like hotcakes.

The goal had always been to build the brand and sell it. In 2010 this finally happened when Proximo Spirits bought the vodka for an undisclosed sum, although St. George continued making it for them until April 2014. When Winters gives a tour, he points out the assembly line where Hangar One is being bottled and packaged. Crates of pears wait to be fermented, and in the middle of the hangar is a giant shark.

A few years ago the company next door, which specialized in digital special effects, asked Winters if he wouldn't mind storing a black shark mold. The shark had been used in the movie *Deep Blue Sea* (starring Thomas Jane, Samuel L. Jackson, and L.L. Cool J). The effects company is gone; the shark remains.

Winters lays out the two ways to market your product, which he calls push or pull. "Most vodkas work on that *push* mentality: We've got a great packaging concept, we've come up with a brilliant story, let's get this product out there. It's cheap to make. Let's put as much of it out there in the market as possible. . . . We'll make sure that for every five cases people buy, they get an additional two of them free so they're

Lance Winters of St. George Spirits—according to his business card, his title is "Evil Genius." *Ben Krantz*

< 191 >

hooked on this stuff, we'll make sure people see Jennifer Aniston drinking it at parties, they'll know that it's cool."

Craft distillers like St. George, on the other hand, opt to *pull* the consumer in, "because they like the way it tastes and they can't make a cocktail with any other product that comes close to it. That was the methodology that we chose to use because that pulls it through the marketplace. . . . I'm not here to sell somebody's packaging skills. I'm here to make a product that I feel great about, something that I feel is an artistic expression, and to have people drink that."

The strategy is working. In 2004 *Atlantic Monthly* columnist Corby Kummer profiled St. George Spirits and called Hangar One "an unusual triumph," describing it as "delicate to the nose, almost watery compared with other premium unflavored vodkas, and distinctly winey and light on the tongue. It has the gentle potency of an eau de vie, and a finesse I found in no other vodka." But will the finesse remain once St. George stops distilling it?

Across the bay, in San Francisco, lies Anchor Distilling, which claims space in the same building as the more popular Anchor Brewery. The tasting room, even at 11:00 a.m., teems with visitors sampling flights of beer. The top-floor office of David King, president of Anchor Distilling, offers an impressive view of the city skyline.

"We're making an outdoor garden area, and then we're going to be planting herbs and fruit up in planters," explains

The St. George Spirits Distillery. *Ben Krantz*

< 194 >

the Scotsman. "I also bought the biggest library of old cocktail books and recipes. . . . I'm going to create a library of these old cocktail books, and we've got the bar behind here. . . . The idea is that you come in, you can look at an original cocktail book from the 1870s, and then re-create that recipe right here. We see this as being a real learning environment."

The Anchor still.
Courtesy of Anchor Distilling Company

King came over from the UK when his company, Berry Brothers & Rudd, invested in Anchor Distilling in 2010, a complex "strategic partnership" deal that involved the Berry Brothers' sale of Cutty Sark whisky.[38]

Although the Anchor Brewing Company has existed since 1896, it was verging on shutting down in the 1960s. But a Stanford University graduate student named Fritz Maytag came to the rescue rather than going into the family appliance business. Maytag started distilling in 1993 but relinquished control of the company in 2010.[39] The Anchor Distilling portfolio

---

38 In its heyday, circa 1979, "Cutty shipped 2.9 million nine-liter cases to the United States," says King. "Today, they do about 150,000."

39 He remains chairman of the board of Maytag Dairy Farms, maker of Maytag Blue Cheese.

< 195 >

Anchor Distillers.
Courtesy of Anchor Distilling Company

includes single malts, rums, tequilas, eaux de vie, and a variety of liqueurs and aperitifs. They make the enormously popular Junipero Gin on premise—but no vodka of which to speak.

"I am personally a little bit anti-vodka," David admits. "It's funny, but it's almost a mentality, and personally I have never drunk vodka. I have never seen the purpose of it. I see it purely as an alcohol delivery vehicle. I don't even like it as a blank canvas."

So how does he explain the vodka boom?

"To me, vodka in a way sums up the whole American palate across all things. That's why McDonald's does so well. That's why light beer does so well. It's just easy. It's accessible. I don't think Americans like to work hard at their

< 196 >

palates particularly. It's changing; it depends where you live. But you like easy. That's why these stupid whipped cream vodkas and all the rest of it—I mean, to me it's ridiculous as a grown man."

And yet.

While sitting at his bar, David confides that "I was really inspired by the smell of hops in the building. . . . Hops is probably one of the biggest flavors in the United States and the world if you think about IPAs and all the rest of it. I managed to get the distillers to work with me" to develop a sort of hop-infused spirit. "You can't do it with all types of hops—certain strains of hops. The guys downstairs were messing with hop varieties for ages. Then the fact that we distilled, not just infused—so we infused and then distilled, that's another part of the secret of how to do it—it's pretty interesting." To say the least. At the time of my visit, it was still pending approval from the Alcohol and Tobacco Tax and Trade Bureau, which ultimately had to assign a spirit designation.

"The production process is very similar to making gin. However, the definition of gin is that it's got to have a predominantly juniper flavor. Then you say, 'Well, although we make it like a gin, it's clearly not a gin because there's no juniper in it,'" King explains. "Calling it a gin would be unfair because the consumer would think he were getting a juniper-flavored product. They go, 'Well, that's definitely flavored; it definitely tastes like gin on the palate. It doesn't behave like a vodka, I don't think.' But it's definitely not juniper so I can't call it gin. So then you say, 'Is it a hop-flavored eau de vie?' Well, no, because it's not made from grapes. It's grain spirits."

< 197 >

A vodka is born: Hophead Vodka by Anchor Distilling.
Courtesy of Anchor Distilling

Not long after my visit, the TTB made its determination: It's vodka.

But King already suspected this. The prototype he showed me featured a label that read "H-V" for Hopped Vodka. He also had a potential name for it: Hophead. "I just felt that Hophead had that whole San Francisco Haight-Ashbury feel, you know? Also, it's very clear. I thought, if there's going to be any problem with what it is, then if I give it a really obvious name, what is it? It's hops."

To date, you can buy Hophead Vodka in thirty-one states.

David calls Anchor's marketing strategy "liquid-led, bartender-endorsed." It sounds familiar. But the Scotsman has a unique way of explaining the importance of recruiting those bartenders: "One of the greatest marketing stories ever of course is Christianity, right? Jesus did it with twelve disciples, and it was word of mouth, and he sent them out. There

The Anchor stills, hard at work. *Courtesy of Anchor Distilling Company*

< 200 >

Death's Door president Brian Ellison and master distiller John Jeffery.
Courtesy of Death's Door Spirits

wasn't any big mass-marketing campaign. Bibles weren't written until way later. This was old guys going around, word of mouth storytelling."

If only vodka could raise people from the dead instead of making them feel like they were at . . .

Death's Door lies about three hours from Chicago, and one of the first things company president Brian Ellison and master distiller John Jeffery will tell you is that the name has nothing to do with death. Rather it comes from the passageway between the Wisconsin mainland and Washington Island, both in Door County.

"It's horribly cheeky," Ellison admits. "We had a group that contacted us—they wanted to do a group Goth wedding in

< 201 >

Transylvania with Marilyn Manson as the presiding minister. I was like, 'No.' They wanted Death's Door at all the tables. . . . There's this whole steampunk thing that's way into Death's Door."

Ellison has a background in economic development, so for him Death's Door was about helping the farming community on Washington Island. "We got to the point where in the 1970s potato farming had died out. There was no way they could scratch a living at farming, so everybody's just living sort of subsistence, and it was becoming a little bit of a poor man's Martha's Vineyard of Chicago, where people would come up and buy a farm and live in the farmhouse and just let the fields go fallow."

The initial plan called for making the wheat from the fields into bread. "We had a lot of attention, but there was just no money in it. It's like trying to save an island on a bake sale." So

Seedling wheat on Washington Island, Wisconsin, harvested for Death's Door.
Courtesy of Death's Door Spirits

The towering column still at Death's Door.
Courtesy of Death's Door Spirits

he turned to alcohol—specifically beer and then vodka. A distiller in Cedar Rapids offered Ellison the use of his 25-gallon electric still, so he had a brewery make him the mash, which he then transported to Iowa to process. "It's three and a half hours in a rental truck with 350 gallons of beer, which is totally illegal by the way."

When the business grew, Ellison opened his own distilling facility. He and John Jeffery had grown tired of dealing with contract manufacturers over neutral grain spirits. "Literally getting into yelling fights with people about what they were 'fixing' about the distillation style," says Jeffery. The contractors see themselves "as artists and as being able to improve on things, and they really don't just want to turn levers and push buttons." But behind all the talk of passion and art and "the craft," that's what happens.

Bottles of Death's Door Vodka, ready to be filled.
Courtesy of Death's Door Spirits

"It always blows people away when we tell them our whiskey and our vodka are essentially made from the same thing," Jeffery says. "It's the same grain mix, it's a little bit different yeast, but all I have to do is throw a couple of switches on the still, and I get one or the other. There're no fireworks. . . . It's two switches, and you've got one product or another, just based on what you're including and not including."

After vodka Ellison decided to try gin. "I'm walking into this vodka minefield or jumping into the deep end of the pool with lots of big sharks. It's a lot more fun to go into the gin kiddie pool, where nobody cares that I play there, and I'm not looking to expand to some huge market share. I just need a corner."

Except that the corner has expanded. From seven hundred cases total the first year, Death's Door now approaches

Death's Door, ready for rollout.
Courtesy of Death's Door Spirits

Death's Door Vodka.
Courtesy of Death's Door Spirits

forty thousand annually. The craft distillery now makes neutral grain spirits for other brands, much as large ethanol plants have been doing for everyone else. At the moment they have only four clients, but that number will grow. "We want them to feel confident that their story can be about the grain that they use and how they make their product," says Ellison. Death's Door, through its Alpha Distillates Program, makes the NGS but allows their clients to do the finishing distillation and provide signature additives.

So can you still call them a craft distiller? Lance Winters would argue: "You can have a really small distillery putting out horrible product. Are they a craft distiller? I don't think so. If somebody is applying sound methodologies using the best quality ingredients they can find and putting out a solidly good product, I don't think it matters whether they're putting out five thousand cases or five hundred thousand—they're still craftspersons."

If Death's Door continues to grow and someone wants to buy them, under the right circumstances Ellison has no problem with this. "It was never a lifestyle decision to start this company. It was: Let's see if we can take this experiment as far as we can and see if we can offer an opportunity to farmers and make things better." But again, he stresses that

< 206 >

a deal would have to be right. "If they can do it in a way that still preserves the integrity of the brand and preserves that they're still working with the farmers on Washington Island . . . I think that most definitely I'll get out of the way and, in fact, would welcome the opportunity to go do something else."

Ellison half-jokingly fears that even with reassurances, "they'll immediately turn and make it about death and dying, make little coffins and put the bottles in little coffins. Then it's going to be like, Yeah, you just frickin' killed it."

The guys at Industry City Distillery, on the other hand, say they can't be bought. The five twentysomethings toiling on

The Industry City Distillery team.
Courtesy of the ICD staff

< 207 >

Dave Kyrejko of Industry City Distillery testing flow.
Courtesy of the ICD staff

the sixth floor of a Brooklyn warehouse, having sold a few
hundred cases of vodka distilled from beet sugar, compose
the unlikeliest group of craft distillers you might come across.
They don't even like to be called craft distillers.

In the old Bush Terminal—a few blocks from the 36th
Street Station, just past the Gowanus Expressway—the distillery shares warehouse space with a Chinese export-import
business involving suitcases. Laborers on the ground floor
push pallets stacked with Equal and Angelo Mia pizza sauce.
Across the way lies a flavoring company called Virginia Dare.
Depending on the day, it smells of grape, cherry, Raisin Bran,
popcorn, and Tootsie Roll.

According to the ICD website, the company consists of "a
printmaking biological engineer and science nerd; a machinist
with a bent for sculpture; a code-wrangling graphic designer

< 208 >

and fabricator; a yoga instructor turned business manager; a hard-working commercial salmon fisherman and a whole lot of yeast." Peter Simon is the yoga instructor turned manager.

Everything is made on premise. The fermentation, distillation, bottling, and packaging all happen on the sixth floor. The place is in a bit of a shambles, sort of like the *Friends* apartment occupied by squatters. But it's organized chaos; everyone knows what he or she is doing and, equally important, the confines of their workspaces—separate areas for machinery, distilling, testing, etc.

The latest from ICD: Industry Standard Vodka. *Courtesy of the ICD staff*

But ICD is perplexing. What do you mean your entire fermentation operation takes up just five by eight feet? What do you mean you distill only twice? How do "esters" (carboxylic acid-derived chemical compounds found in natural oils) determine the flavor of your vodka?

Even how they coalesced is odd. Distiller Dave Kyrejko had the idea to build a giant fish tank, in which the plant life would provide oxygen for fish. "But there weren't enough fish in there to produce enough CO_2 for the plants," Peter Simon explains, "so he ended up doing fermentation to inject CO_2 into the system. The byproduct of that was alcohol, so he started looking into the alcohol. How can we make this

< 209 >

Vodkas One and Two at ICD.
Courtesy of the ICD staff

usable? That was kind of the process of how we started looking into distillation."

They didn't ask for help, either from outside investors
or even guidance from the American Distillers Association.
"Dave opens up his physics textbook and is looking into distillation," says Simon. "The thing that pops up when you're
looking at how to get the best separation of alcohol compounds is a packed column and to distill fractionally. So he
built a fractional rig."

Simple as that.

Kyrejko elaborates: "Instead of thinking in traditional
terms of heads, hearts, and tails, and redistilling, this takes
that entire thing and throws it out the window and looks
directly at scientific and industrial distillation. . . . Instead of

< 210 >

us thinking, *We're going to go pretend that we're moonshiners or something,* we just look at the industrial and scientific world where they have no choice but to be incredibly exacting. Really it's nothing new."

But in the craft distilling universe, it is. After all, who else in the United States is distilling vodka from *beets*? "As compared with corn, beets are drastically more efficient at using the land, using energy," says Kyrejko. "The byproducts are more useful. The energy density is higher. Why would we not use sugar beets?"

Then comes the question of why so few cases. Until recently the guys handled the distribution themselves. Simon had been making deliveries by car. But what little they've made has sold out. "It's been so easy for us to sell based on the fact that it's from Brooklyn, people love local products, it's fucking delicious. Then people want to keep us around because this is actually good, which is really nice."

It sounds like they've just found the motto for their fourth vodka. Industry Standard Vodka: It's fucking delicious.

And it is.

14

THE MIDDLE KINGDOM

Ketel One was the first brand to sting us.
—RICHARD W. LEWIS, FORMER ABSOLUT WORLDWIDE
ACCOUNT DIRECTOR, TBWA\CHIAT\DAY

When TBWA's Geoff Hayes and Graham Turner came up with the Absolut Perfection ad in 1980, little did they know that it would spawn more than two thousand variations spanning two decades. On April 1, 1997, Absolut ran a fake ad announcing that "the most popular ad campaign of all time need not run for all time." It contained descriptions about the wheat and the distilling process but no clever imagery reflecting the iconic bottle.[40] But the end was near.

In *Absolut Sequel: The Absolut Advertising Story Continues,* former TBWA executive Richard W. Lewis explains the purpose of Absolut Perfection: "Yes, we wanted you to smile

---

[40] If you called the toll-free number in the ad, a recording explained that it was a hoax.

< 213 >

when you recognize the halo of an angel, but it's the bottle and its contents that are 'perfect.'" Then he asks rhetorically, "Seriously, is there a level of quality higher than that?"

That was the problem. How do you get more perfect than perfection?

Absolut's marketing strategy began to falter around 1995. New competitors and old rivals threatened its position either by offering quality at a cheaper price or claiming to be better and costing more. "Ketel One was the first brand to sting us," writes Lewis. Then came Grey Goose, more expensive than both Absolut and Ketel, along with Belvedere, Chopin, Effen, and the rest, all super-premium, higher-priced brands that the bartenders placed on the top shelf.

"Each brand wanted to grow big by emphasizing they were small," Lewis writes. He acknowledges that these companies, which stress that they are "distilled in small batches" and "handcrafted" and "old-world recipes" succeeded in "driving Absolut down the hierarchy." Add to this the rise of artisanal spirits—actually distilled in small batches and handcrafted—which drew the attention of hipster bars, and the vodka from Sweden was facing a serious problem.

For Absolut, something had to be done to stop this downward slide, a predicament familiar to SKYY. But walk into any bar today, and you won't find Absolut on the top shelf. In fact, Brian Ellison of Death's Door claims, "It's hardly even an on-premise product anymore. It's almost all liquor stores."

An exaggeration perhaps, but how much truth was in Ellison's statement?

Who better to consult than Adam Stagliano, chief strategy officer for TBWA. Although based in London, Stagliano

< 214 >

Adam Stagliano, chief international strategy officer for TBWA Worldwide:
The man does not mince words. *Courtesy of Jamie Sadd*

came to New York to deal with another TBWA client. Located on Madison Avenue and 52nd Street, the TBWA offices take up three floors of the legendary Look Building, named after former tenant *Look* magazine. This Modernist white-brick complex is where Bob Dylan recorded "The Times, They Are a Changin'." But unlike the aging exterior, the interior of TBWA feels bright and open. Two-story windows offer a full-height view of St. Patrick's Cathedral.

The employees don't resemble anyone you'd see on *Mad Men*—no one in a suit and tie—but they share a similar wardrobe. For the men it's all about layers: an undershirt beneath a pink button-down beneath a sweater or fleece beneath a blazer, and possibly a scarf, above designer jeans above really nice shoes. Everyone sports thick-framed glasses and carefully messed-up hair. One man was wearing pastel green pants, and he didn't look out of place.

Stagliano, on the other hand, is wearing a white-cotton dress shirt and a navy blazer. Bespectacled and with flowing, almost shoulder-length graying hair, he looks a little like comedian Richard Lewis; he even puts his fingers to his forehead from time to time. Living in London has had no effect on his Philly accent.

"Absolut put the vodka movement on steroids," Stagliano declares. "It was the first brand that didn't just recognize, it leaned into and then leveraged popular culture. Lots of brands talk about, We gotta be part of the culture, we gotta get into the culture. Absolut did it. It leaned in, and then it created its own. We can talk about lots of different strategies, but fundamentally it was curating culture and branding the

< 216 >

culture with the word Absolut. I can say this because I wasn't a part of it, but it was fuckin' pure genius."

In December 2012 Absolut announced that Sid Lee Entertainment, whose clients include Cirque du Soleil, would share advertising duties with TBWA. Or as *Adweek* put it: "Sid Lee has knocked TBWA off its perch as lead global creative agency on Absolut." Bertrand Cesvet, chairman of Sid Lee, said, "We know that in a world in which advertising is all too often wallpaper, we need to do something different. We have to engage the consumer in experiences and demonstrate the purpose of the brand."

Wallpaper? Was he getting in a dig at Absolut's ads, which adorned so many dorm room walls?

"Yeah, I was fucking surprised," says Stagliano with refreshing candor. "We're still nominally in charge of the fucking global strategy, so I'm still back and forth from Stockholm all the time. We'll see where Sid Lee goes. I'm sure they played a card about 'experiential'—what they did for Cirque du Soleil, as though that has any relationship—but that's just me." He also clarifies that "they didn't replace us as the global agency. They were added to the roster. But for your purposes, the history of vodka and everything, it's a blip. It might not be a blip inside this building, 488 Madison."[41] Looking back on those brilliant ads, had Absolut become a prisoner of its own genius? "People have said that," Stagliano admits. "I don't know how many campaigns can run for twenty-five years, so

---

41 The account transferred to TBWA's London office.

< 217 >

if we ran into a cul-de-sac it was a pretty fucking long cul-de-sac. I mean, twenty-five years. People say it became a box. Well, the box then was gargantuan."

But to this day, he adds, "We still never put an idea on the table to beat that. There has been interesting stuff that has been done. But nothing has beat the campaign, and to be honest, to a certain extent, clients and agency over the years got more tired of it than people in the world did—literally people in the rest of the world." He's referring to places like Brazil, where Absolut reigns more popular than ever. "It's still in a way brand new. They [Brazilians] don't have the twenty-five or thirty years of baggage."

Likewise, China doesn't have three decades of baggage, either. The problem, Stagliano points out, is that the country also lacks a cocktail culture. "There are certain countries where you don't mix stuff and other cultures where you do mix." Mixing promotes cocktail culture, and the ultimate mixer is vodka. As a result, China remains predominantly a brown-spirits nation, which is good news for Pernod Ricard brands Chivas, Martell, and Royal Salute. "I don't know where the next generation's going to go with it, but vodka doesn't seem naturally to fit Chinese culture, to be honest. They'll mix whiskey with green tea, but they don't have a cocktail culture."

As for the competition: "You gotta take your hats off to what Grey Goose has done. They completely outflanked

The ultramodern lobby at TBWA's midtown Manhattan offices.
Bill Hornstein

< 220 >

Absolut. They became the new super-premium." Then Sta-gliano presciently addresses my biggest concern: "You got the Grey Goose and all the Grey Goose emulators. Then you have a leader, the one who used to be out front of the pack being squeezed in the fucking middle. The middle is no place to be in a lot of businesses. But it's *death* in the spirits business."

They do see a way out, though. Absolut still ranks as the top imported vodka in the United States. It's expanding into other countries around the world, and it has introduced a new and viable product, Absolut Elyx.

According to promotional material, Absolut Elyx "is made using a single year's harvest of the highest quality Swed-ish winter wheat," not unlike Ketel One's ultra-wheat, by the sound of it. "The unique properties of the copper column still greatly contribute to the incomparable purity of Absolut Elyx. Inside, the copper surfaces have a catalytic effect on some of the trace compounds in the spirit, resulting in a naturally pure vodka." Even Dave Kyrejko of Industry City Distillery acknowl-edges the inherent value of copper in distillation.

The dilemma, though, says Stagliano, is that "for thirty years you're out there saying you are the perfect vodka. Are you actually saying this is *more* perfect? It's a strange situ-ation." Then he referred me to his friend Martin Riley, chief marketing officer for Pernod Ricard.

Martin and I met a few months later at the Algonquin Hotel, home to the "Vicious Circle" of *New Yorker* writers includ-ing Dorothy Parker, Robert Benchley, and Alexander Wooll-cott. A cheery Englishman in his fifties, Martin Riley began at Sandeman, the sherry and port company, before joining the

< 221 >

The famous Råbelöf estate wheat, used exclusively for Absolut Elyx.
Phil Barton

Seagram empire until its dissolution at the hands of Diageo, Pernod Ricard, and Vivendi in 2000. Riley happened to be in New York in his capacity as president of the World Federation of Advertisers, and he tells of a funny idea ginned up by the Swedes.

"They were getting fed up with advertising," Riley says, so "they ran a campaign saying, Fed up with advertising? Imagine a world where there is no advertising and win a trip to a place where there is no advertising—North Korea."

Maybe not such a funny idea.

"It was real," Riley insists. "They ran it on the website, they had some great visuals, and they're showing Pyongyang, where there is no advertising—and no people, either. Two

< 222 >

Absolut Elyx.
Fredrik Boman, Andreas Sjöstrand

Absolut Elyx, served—properly—on the rock. *Fredrik Boman, Andreas Sjöstrand*

people won the trip, but they couldn't go because it was just at the time where there was recent trouble, so they're going in September [2013]."

Such a sense of humor, those Swedes! On the other hand, they're taking Absolut Elyx very seriously. "It's being very targeted. It's going right to the top accounts," says Riley, by which he means the hottest bars in New York and Miami, and "opinion-leading liquor stores" as well. "The reception from the bartenders has been fantastic because it delivers on taste."

< 224 >

Not only that, it also comes with a ritual. "They've got a very big square piece of ice, round glass, and you pour it over the ice. You drink it through the ice, and it's a fantastic way of drinking it. To have a ritual, a great-tasting product with a story behind why it's so tasty, how it comes out of the original copper stills, and then you have the packaging, which is knockout packaging"—how could it miss?[42]

Of course skeptics abound. Brian Ellison of Death's Door says with a laugh, "I haven't tried it, but I don't need to try it. Everybody gets it, you know what I mean? It's like, Hey, let's make this, and then we're going to take that down, and now we've got this!" A European distiller also poked fun at Absolut's "winter wheat" claim. "Most European wheat [used in distilling] is winter wheat because it's just easier to grind than summer wheat."

Naturally, Martin Riley has a less cynical take. "Can you get out of the middle?" he asks. "What you can do in a market like America is say, Hey, we produced something that's sufficiently different to our core mother brand but takes the values, takes the quality, the heritage, everything else from the mother brand, and it gets people to reappraise it. By reappraising it, it doesn't mean to say they're never going to drink Absolut Blue or one of the flavored ones again—just: 'Wow, this is a very special vodka. I'm going to go back and . . . you know, I used to drink Absolut, maybe I'm going to drink it again.' That's the strategy."

---

42 Running out of large square ice.

< 225 >

A waiter comes to take our drink order. Martin asks for Absolut, but the Algonquin Hotel doesn't carry it or Pernod's other vodka, Wyborowa. He seems mildly disappointed, though the revelation would have come as no surprise to Brian Ellison. But as chief marketing officer, Riley has the entire portfolio memorized and requests a Beefeater and tonic.

Then he explains that when Beefeater came to the United States, it was twice the price of local gin. The same, he says, with Chivas, which was more expensive than other Scotches at the time. Absolut, of course, became the most expensive vodka in America until Ketel One arrived. So what Grey Goose did was nothing new. "You can take big steps in terms of pricing as long as you're supporting it with a good proposition, substance, why you're asking for this much more money. Those [overpriced] brands that don't substantiate it, it doesn't work. They can sit on the shelf because they're expensive and there's no 'why,' or someone might buy it once as a novelty."

Riley believes Elyx is a good proposition and has substance. Judges at the 2013 San Francisco World Spirits Competition agreed. In a blind taste test, they voted it the unanimous winner: Double Gold.

Hope springs eternal.

< 226 >

EPILOGUE

Why doesn't Poland Spring make a vodka?

—FOCUS GROUP PARTICIPANT TO

TBWA's Richard Lewis

On May 22, 2013, New Jersey liquor authorities raided twenty-nine bars and restaurants across the state, seizing a thousand bottles, as part of Operation Swill. A number of establishments, including eight T.G.I. Friday's locations, had been filling top-shelf bottles with cheap rail. One place even substituted rubbing alcohol and caramel coloring for Scotch. Another was using the equivalent of dirty river water. Officials investigated bottles of Absolut, Finlandia, Grey Goose, Ketel One, and Smirnoff.

In Europe the situation was worse. A criminal ring in England had been selling hundreds of thousands of counterfeit bottles of Glen's Vodka containing bleach and methanol. Drinking methanol can cause blindness. The *New York Times* reported that in the Czech Republic, more than twenty people died after consuming tainted liquor.

Alcohol abuse continues to hammer Russia. Within forty years, the United Nations estimates, the nation's population will drop by thirty million. Life expectancy has fallen to 69.7

years, as opposed to 83 in nearby Japan. "The Russians have fought off many enemies, from Napoleon to Hitler, and the men who led them in those fights earned chapters in the history books," writes Oliver Bullough in the *Wall Street Journal.* "But Mr. Putin will be remembered as the man who failed to defend the Russians against the most terrible enemy of all: their own love of vodka."

While researching and writing this book, I came across news stories of underage students eating Gummi Bears soaked in vodka, college kids doing "eyeball shots" to get drunk faster, and even one report about vodka-dipped tampons. About the only good news came in December 2012 when two circus elephants, stranded in forty-below temperatures in Novosibirsk, Russia, and facing certain death, were kept warm with two cases of vodka. An official told *Ria Novosti,* "They started roaring like if they were in the jungle!"

You might think that by now we would've gotten sick of vodka. But you'd be wrong. In 2002 we purchased thirty-nine million cases of it. In 2012 that number shot to sixty-five million cases. One reason, says Brian Ellison, is that vodka is vanilla ice cream.

"Anybody who makes ice cream has a vanilla because vanilla is the number one seller," explains the owner of Death's Door. "But every vanilla is not the same. When people say vodka is vodka, that's like saying vanilla ice cream is vanilla ice cream. Häagen-Dazs is different than Ben & Jerry's is different than Italian gelato. But at the same time, everybody makes a vodka because everybody buys a vodka."

Brian extends the analogy: Ice cream makers get most of their mix from a handful of dairy companies. The brands can

< 228 >

add butterfat and air afterward to distinguish their product from others. Similarly, most vodka makers get their neutral grain spirits from a few select processors, such as Distilled Resources Inc., Chippewa Valley Ethanol Company, and Grain Processing Corporation. They can add citric acid, vanillin, and sugar later.

But Ellison's right: Vodka isn't vodka. The famous *New York Times* blind taste test—in which twenty-one leading vodka brands went head to head and Smirnoff came out on top—didn't mean they were all the same but that our preferences may be less top shelf than we think.[43] So it's partly a matter of taste. The late art director at the magazine where I work, a Russian named Lev Nisnevitch, drank only Swedish Absolut. "Stoli is *sheet,*" he said in his thick accent. Yet others apparently prefer the *sheet.* In one taste test I preferred SKYY over Ketel One, in another, Ketel over Absolut and Grey Goose.

But should vodka have flavor or have craft distillers and super-premiums exerted undue influence? The makers of Ketel One and Absolut Elyx encourage us to drink vodka on the rocks or with one big square block of ice, and as David Embury sagely observed in 1958: "If you don't like the taste of liquor, why drink it?" But this nevertheless would mark a serious shift in our drinking habits, since vodka on ice is still largely viewed as dipsomaniacal.

---

43 Max Watman, author of *Chasing the White Dog,* relates how he and a group of whiskey aficionados mistook a two-year-old Indian malt for a sixteen-year-old Oban. "We weren't ashamed or insulted to learn its true provenance, just happy for the surprise, and happy to learn about another excellent whiskey in the world."

Despite Embury's rhetorical injunction, many drinkers don't want to taste their booze. "As [classic cocktails] underwent a vodka conversion, the rising generation discovered that vodka served its purposes ideally," writes William Grimes in *Straight Up or On the Rocks*. "Teenagers consume alcohol with the goal of getting drunk. The fewer obstacles in the way, the better, and acquired taste is an obstacle. . . . With vodka, the cocktail shed all its complications overnight, becoming nothing more than a goosed-up fruit drink—Hawaiian punch with sting."

Having run countless focus groups for more than twenty years, TBWA's Richard Lewis came to his own conclusion: "What taste do you prefer in a vodka? Vodka with no taste. No smell. No burn. No nothing. . . . You want vodka that tastes like water! Or, as close as it possibly can." One focus group participant actually asked, "Why doesn't Poland Spring make a vodka?"[44]

If many of us want our vodka to taste like water, how to choose? Does the brand convey status? What's the backstory? How many times is it distilled? Is it charcoal-filtered? Diamond-filtered? What about the packaging? Grey Goose "looks fantastic behind the bar," writes *New York* magazine's Seth Stevenson, "the way it catches light. . . . It looks expensive."

---

44 There is in fact a Poland Spring vodka, produced by White Rock Distilleries—which Beam Global sold to Sazerac in October 2013—not to be confused with Poland Spring water, owned by Nestlé. Both products take their water from the Poland Spring in Maine.

< 230 >

Roman Kaplan of the Russian Samovar in New York told an anecdote of how he and his wife were recently in Florida at a restaurant that only served wine and beer. "They said there's a store next door, so I went down there and I bought the most beautiful bottle without thinking because I figured if they can produce such interesting bottles, then it must be good, successful. I brought this vodka [Beluga]. There were four of us. We drank the whole bottle straight."

Packaging works—even on the Russians! Though, to be fair, they were drinking it straight, which also counts for something.

But that sort of psychology drives Adam Stagliano crazy. TBWA's chief strategy officer points to Michel Roux, one of the creative geniuses behind Absolut, as being inadvertently responsible for "shifting the way everybody in the spirits business looked at marketing, for good and evil. For good, he definitely taught people the value of popular culture. For evil, he taught a lot of people that product doesn't matter." But that line of thinking is misleading, says Stagliano. "A lesson drawn from what they *thought* Roux was doing—I should clarify—with their product is it doesn't matter." What he means is that Absolut's advertising campaign enhanced an already sound product. A blinking LED light at the bottom of a bottle, on the other hand . . .

Toward the end of my research, I dropped in to see Robert Birnecker at Koval again. It had been two years since our last meeting, and the business was no longer fledgling. Birnecker, though with less hair and looking a bit more tired, was upbeat. He gave me a tour of the second facility—including an additional ten thousand square feet of production area—and told

< 231 >

The new Koval stills, bigger and better.
Courtesy of Koval

me that new Kothe stills with larger capacity were coming shortly. His boys, five and three, now drive toy cars around the distillery.

Like Death's Door, Koval provides neutral grain spirits for a few clients, and they have gone from having four employees to thirteen. But the most astounding change took place in overall volume: From four thousand cases in 2009 to twenty-five thousand cases four years later. You can buy Koval products in twenty-seven states now, plus Europe and Australia. He's come a long way from those eighteen-hour days and

Robert Birnecker prepares for the new stills at Koval.
Courtesy of Koval

< 233 >

nights working alone and realizing that he'd taken "a plunge off the very deep end."

"I was just thinking that today," Birnecker says. "I walked past our barrel station, and there were twelve barrels there getting watered and primed for filling. I thought, *What, this is all we have right now?*—and I was serious. In that second, I was like, '*Wow.*' When we filled our first barrels in 2009, I thought, *Oh, we finally have three barrels!* It took us forever to make those three barrels. Now I'm like, 'What, you're only filling twelve?'"

Koval Vodka, its bottles getting a face-lift, now accounts for just 15 percent of output. Everything else is booming. Birnecker just inked a deal with the Ritz-Carlton and Marriott hotels for them to carry his two hundred-milliliter bottles of whiskey in their suites, allowing for a more generous pour than those nip bottles currently in the minibar.

"I think everybody is underestimating the distribution aspect. Making the product is one thing," Birnecker says. "But then selling it and getting it placed and making it interesting for bartenders and for the consumers is difficult. A lot of people have absolutely no connection with the end-consumer. They get on the shelf, and nobody buys them. It's not even about the quality of their product. It's just that they can't do anything with it. They believe that once they've sold it to the distributor, their job ends right at their door, and it never does."

Robert explains all this and more at his distilling seminars. Koval now runs five a year, each with forty attendees who travel from all over the world and pay $799 for the three-day course. That comes to roughly $160,000 in additional income. "They have fueled our growth," Birnecker admits. "But it's also helped the industry because the original idea was, We don't

< 234 >

Like a proud father, Robert Birnecker stands in front of his whiskey barrels at Koval. *Courtesy of Koval*

want people going out using Kothe equipment producing crappy product. Then it extended into: We don't want people using any equipment making crappy product because, if you try one craft product that's bad, you'll assume every craft product is bad."

But Birnecker remains hopeful about the future of the industry: "There's still room to grow for the right people and for people who do things properly." His other colleagues offer varied assessments.

"It's here to stay, but it's not going to continue the trajectory that it's had," says Lance Winters of St. George Spirits.

< 235 >

"More and more people are exploring spirits. You're seeing more and more spirit-driven cocktails. If you've got a cocktail driven by a spirit, you're going to need something that's full flavored, not full *of* flavor. So you start to see bartenders looking at the old Jerry Thomas books, *The Bon Vivant's Companion,* things like that, for their cocktail inspiration. There's no vodka in there. It's all whiskey, brandy, gin."

"Vodka is America's spirit," counters Maura McGinn of SKYY. "There's also big demographic shifts happening in the category. Females have always been welcome, and now you've got a lot more ethnicities going into vodka. There's also that movement of lower-calorie. It can mix with everything, so by being the most flexible spirit it will always grow."

Distillers ask themselves that question all the time: Who will want to drink *our* product and why? But do we even know as a nation what we want from our vodka? For a growing number of consumers, it's becoming more about texture, mouthfeel, even creaminess, a sure sign that Americans are, in fact, working harder on their palates—despite David King's criticism. But the contingent that wants alcoholic bottled water remains sizable.

Part of the Koval three-day course includes a sensory seminar. The attendees, says Birnecker, "just get numbers. We put a craft vodka, a contract-distilled vodka, Absolut, Svedka . . . we put the whole lineup, and we let people vote." In one course, "100 percent, everybody liked the Wolfschmidt."

So maybe we want affordability but don't want to admit it? A 1.75-liter bottle of Wolfschmidt sells for fourteen dollars. It's a deal if you don't mind that it comes in a plastic jug and hasn't been poured over a model's breasts.

< 236 >

APPENDIX
THE VODKA BOOM

America's thirst for vodka is unquenchable. More than 65 million nine-liter cases of vodka were sold here in 2012, totaling $5.5 billion in distiller revenues. Not only are we Americans drinking more vodka annually, but we're willing to spend more on super-premium brands. The volume in that category alone increased by 10 percent in just one year. The flavorless, odorless, colorless spirit commands a staggering 32 percent of the entire spirits market—more than whiskey, rum, or tequila.

Also, as much as some may hate them, flavored vodkas continue to remain popular, comprising 21 percent of all vodkas sold and growing by 19 percent in the span of a year. Cinnabon martini, anyone?

< 237 >

U.S. VODKA MARKET

Volumes by Year and Price Category
9-Liter Cases

Year	Value Brands	Premium	High-End Premium	Super Premium	Grand Total	Supplier Revenue
2003	20.1 million	10.5 million	9.3 million	1.9 million	41.9 million	$3 billion
2004	20.8 million	10.8 million	9.9 million	2.6 million	44.1 million	$3.3 billion
2005	21.1 million	11.3 million	10.5 million	2.3 million	45.9 million	$3.6 billion
2006	21.1 million	12.3 million	11.2 million	4.1 million	48.8 million	$4 billion
2007	21.9 million	13 million	11.7 million	4.7 million	51.2 million	$4.3 billion
2008	22.5 million	14.7 million	11.6 million	4.6 million	53.3 million	$4.5 billion
2009	24.5 million	15.5 million	11.3 million	4.3 million	56 million	$4.6 billion
2010	25.8 million	16.8 million	11.7 million	5 million	59.4 million	$4.8 billion
2011	26.1 million	18.6 million	12.1 million	5.7 million	62.7 million	$5.2 billion
2012	26.6 million	19.8 million	12.5 million	6.3 million	65.2 million	$5.5 billion

Source: Distilled Spirits Council's Economic & Strategic Analysis Department

9-LITER CASES SOLD

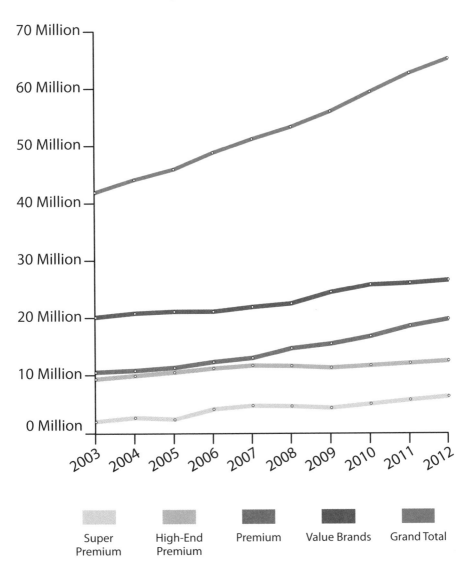

ACKNOWLEDGMENTS

Over the past year, more than a few people gave me funny looks when I told them I was writing a book about vodka. Some thought I was joking. This, however, cannot be said of my agent, Stacey Glick, at Dystel & Goderich Literary Management, and my editor at Lyons Press, James Jayo. Thanks for taking the idea seriously while knowing we could have a lot of fun putting this together. James's editing, along with that of project editor Julie Marsh, was indispensable.

There wasn't nearly as much drinking as you'd imagine—except at the Russian Samovar where I did nine shots of infused vodka. I wouldn't have been doing shots with owner Roman Kaplan at all if the late Lev Nisnevitch hadn't brought us together.

Frank Coleman of the Distilled Spirits Council of the United States was integral in helping me gain access to the industry. In addition, DISCUS chief economist David Ozgo was helpful in crunching the numbers. I am also indebted to those in the business who answered my calls and e-mails, gave me photo permissions, and arranged for interviews, especially Björn von Matérn and Martin Vigerland at Absolut, Amy Federman at Bacardi, Katie Beer at Lambesis, Lizzie Dewhurst at TBWA, Barry Becton, Sari Brecher, and Jamie Hakim at Diageo, Ellie

Winters at St. George Spirits, Nicole Portwood at Tito's Hand-made Vodka, Ansleigh Westfall at Meg Connolly Communications, and Meghan O'Brien at Anchor Distilling. Trent R. Teyema and Donald Codling were just as helpful in connecting me with Jonathan Hemi and Kristina Arnold at Crystal Head Vodka.

Reporting from California was made possible in part through the Hoover Institution at Stanford University. While visiting Ketel One in Holland, I was fortunate to stay with my sister's in-laws, Leo and Wineke Delhaas of Papendrecht. Likewise, thanks to my aunt Dolores Lim for letting me over-night at her apartment during my interviews in New York City.

I'm thankful for the understanding of my editors at the *Weekly Standard,* namely Bill Kristol, Fred Barnes, Richard Starr, and Claudia Anderson. My colleagues Andrew Ferguson, Christopher Caldwell, Jonathan V. Last, and Matt Labash were, as usual, fonts of wisdom and encouragement. Thanks to Kelly Jane Torrance for picking up the slack during my leave, Philip Terzian for running "Vodka Nation" in his Books & Arts section, and Philip Chalk for guidance on acquiring photos and illustrations.

Outside the office, I am grateful for the advice of Phyllis Richman, my food-writing mentor, Robert Messenger of the *Wall Street Journal,* David Skinner of *Humanities* magazine, H. W. Brands at the University of Texas at Austin, Matthew Continetti of the *Washington Free Beacon,* and Steven Ustaris, not only one of my best friends but also an advertising guru who helped me by deftly translating ad-speak into English.

Needless to say I wouldn't even be in this profession if John Podhoretz hadn't hired me in the first place at the

< 241 >

Weekly Standard before he moved on to the *New York Post* and *Commentary*.

Thanks of course to all my friends who provided inspiration for this book—usually over drinks—including Todd Palladino, John Buckley, Steven Rushford, Steven Schmitt, George Guattare, Sue Moroney, Rich Covey, Peter Loh, Brian Potts, Jose Gil, and Keith Baron.

I am most appreciative of the support of my parents, Victorino and Leticia Matus, and my in-laws, Robert and Linda Dwyer, as well as Steven and Christine Delhaas and Bill and Erin Dwyer.

Writing a book while raising toddlers was no easy task. Many days I saw my son, Michael, and my daughter, Sabrina, only in the mornings, and I went stretches at a time without seeing them at all while traveling. None of this would've been feasible if not for my wife, Kate, to whom this book is dedicated. She didn't complain once and was a constant voice of encouragement. Maybe it helped that I kept bringing home bottles of vodka.

< 242 >

SELECT BIBLIOGRAPHY

Brands, H. W. *The Age of Gold: The California Gold Rush and the New American Dream.* New York: Doubleday, 2002.

Curtis, Wayne. *And a Bottle of Rum: A History of the New World in Ten Cocktails.* New York: Three Rivers Press, 2006.

Embury, David A. *The Fine Art of Mixing Drinks.* New York: Doubleday, 1961.

Fleming, Ian. *Casino Royale.* Las Vegas: Thomas & Mercer, 2012.

Grimes, William. *Straight Up or On the Rocks: The Story of the American Cocktail.* New York: North Point Press, 2001.

Hamilton, Carl. *Absolut: Biography of a Bottle.* New York: Texere, 2000.

Herlihy, Patricia. *The Alcoholic Empire: Vodka and Politics in Late Imperial Russia.* New York: Oxford University Press, 2002.

Himelstein, Linda. *The King of Vodka: The Story of Pyotr Smirnov and the Upheaval of an Empire.* New York: Harper, 2009.

Kanbar, Maurice. *Secrets from an Inventor's Notebook: How to Turn a Good Idea into a Fortune.* New York: Penguin Compass, 2001.

< 243 >

Lewis, Richard W. *Absolut Book: The Absolut Vodka Advertising Story.* North Clarendon, VT: Journey Editions, 1996.

———. *Absolut Sequel: The Absolut Advertising Story Continues.* North Clarendon, VT: Periplus Editions, 2005.

Moore, Roger. *Bond on Bond: Reflections on 50 Years of James Bond Movies.* Guilford, CT: Lyons Press, 2012.

Thomas, Jerry. *How to Mix Drinks, or The Bon Vivant's Companion.* New York: SoHo Books, 2009.

Watman, Max. *Chasing the White Dog: An Amateur Outlaw's Adventures in Moonshine.* New York: Simon & Schuster, 2010.

Wilson, Jason. *Boozehound: On the Trail of the Rare, the Obscure, and the Overrated in Spirits.* Berkeley: Ten Speed Press, 2010.

< 244 >

INDEX

< 245 >

< 246 >

< 248 >

< 249 >

< 250 >

< 251 >